A Glossary of Research Concepts and Issues

By
Dan Remenyi

More than 800 essential concepts and issues required for successful academic research

A Glossary of Research Concepts and Issues
Copyright ©2021, the Author

All rights reserved. Except for the quotation of short passages for the purposes of critical review or use in research, no part of this publication may be reproduced in any material form (including photocopying or storing in any medium by electronic means and whether or not transiently or incidentally to some other use of this publication) without the written permission of the copyright holder except in accordance with the provisions of the Copyright Designs and Patents Act 1988, or under the terms of a licence issued by the Copyright Licensing Agency Ltd, Saffron House, 6-10 Kirby Street, London EC1N 8TS. Applications for the copyright holder's written permission to reproduce any part of this publication should be addressed to the publishers.

Disclaimer: While every effort has been made by the author and the publishers to ensure that all the material in this book is accurate and correct at the time of going to press, any error made by readers as a result of any of the material, formulae or other information in this book is the sole responsibility of the reader. Readers should be aware that the URLs quoted in the book may change or be damaged by malware between the time of publishing and accessing by readers.

ISBN (Print): 978-1-912764-89-1
ISBN (Digital): 978-1-912764-90-7

Cover photograph from Pixabay: https://pixabay.com/photos/library-books-knowledge-information-1147815/

Published by Academic Conferences and Publishing International Limited, Reading, RG4 9SJ, United Kingdom.
dan.remenyi@academic-publishing.org

Available from www.academic-bookshop.com

Contents

	Preface	ii
	About the author	iv
A	A posteriori to Axiom	1
B	Basic Research to Bursary	19
C	Capacity to consent to Cum Laude	25
D	Data to Duty of Care	51
E	EDAMBA to Eyeballing the Data	73
F	Facebook to Fuzzy logic	87
G	Gatekeeper to Guess	97
H	Halo effect to Hypothetico-deductive research	103
I	Ibid to ISSN	111
J	Jargon to Journal	123
K	Key informant to Knowledgeable informant	125
L	Leading question to Longitudinal research	129
M	Mail questionnaires to Multivariate analysis	135
N	Narrative to NVIVO	151
O	Obfuscate to Oxymoron	157
P	Page layout and font sizes to Puzzle solving	165
Q	Qual to Questionnaire protocol	187
R	Radical scepticism to Role playing	189
S	Sample to Systematic literature review	211
T	Tabula rasa to Twitter	233
U	Unacceptable language to Useable returned questionnaire	243
V	Valid argument to Vulnerable participants	247
W	Warranted assertions to Writing style	253
X, Y, Z	X-axis to Z-Score	257

Preface

Learning the vocabulary of academic research is the first step for many individuals on their journey to become a successful academic researcher. It is an important step and for some individuals it can appear to be a substantial hurdle.

Furthermore, it is not a hurdle over which a novice researcher can spring in one giant leap. There are many concepts to come to terms with and there are also many process issues to learn about. In addition, academic research is an evolving endeavour; new ideas, concepts and processes are regularly being added and it is necessary to keep up with this vocabulary.

This dictionary offers 800+ terms and concepts which students and their supervisors will find essential. It will also be of value to other researchers who want to expand their horizon into new or different aspects of their research activities.

There are two approaches to producing a dictionary. The first is to develop a definitive description of the words and terms and then to supply them with full academic references where applicable. This is the encyclopaedic approach. The second way is to produce a series of high level or more generally accessible descriptions of the words and terms without the references, which give the reader the gist of the issues involved, and this could be described as the "ready-reckoner" approach. Readers who want more will need to consult suitable academic sources, of which there are many. This dictionary takes the second route.

Some of the concepts and issues described in this dictionary are challenging to express in a small number of words. Furthermore, there are different points of view which will place emphasis differently on some of these words and terms. It is the fact that there are many different points of view in academic research that makes it such an interesting field in which to work.

There is a word of caution concerning the use of newly encountered words and terms. Over the years I have found that there is a tendency among some newcomers to academic research to learn a new word and to feel that they have immediately fully understood it and all its ramifications. This is seldom the case. Academic concepts often require time to be fully digested and to develop and mature in the thinking of researchers. In general, academic research is quite demanding and it just takes time for the penny to drop.

An example of this occurred recently where a doctoral degree candidate on hearing the definition of a positivist and a constructivist declared herself to be a constructivist. At a subsequent colloquium, when she made this declaration and was asked a few questions about constructivism her obvious ignorance of the subject was highly embarrassing. Perhaps there should be a health warning on words which could read, "Let the speaker (and of course the writer) beware". In the case of using new words which represent new ideas it is perhaps better to hesitate a little rather than rush in.

It is appropriate to mention my use of Wikipedia. Wikipedia is shunned by academics. It is regarded as a highly unreliable source of information. However, whilst I would not regard it as a source whose verisimilitude should be unquestioned, it is quite a useful source of initial information on many topics. Thus, I have made reference to it a number of times in this work. As most readers will appreciate no researcher should accept a single source as being the only or best explanation of anything.

Finally, it is inevitable that a book like this reflects the interests of the author. I will allow readers to come to their own conclusions as to where my interests lie.

Professor Dan Remenyi
dan.remenyi@gmail.com
March 2021

About the author

After completing an MBA Dan Remenyi spent 15 years in business as an ICT consultant before undertaking a PhD. Since obtaining his doctorate he has held a variety of visiting professorships in the United Kingdom, the Republic of Ireland and South Africa. He originally researched and taught in the ICT management field, but for the past decade he has increasingly focussed on research methodology and the sociology of research. He has had some 30 text books published. Some of his books have been translated into Chinese, Japanese and Romanian.

He holds a BSocSc MBA and PhD.

Other relevant research titles authored or co-authored include: -

Case Study Research
Field Methods for Academic Research
Writing up your research
An Introduction to Statistics using Excel
Research Protocols and Research Ethics Committees
Research Supervision for Supervisors and their Students
Grounded Theory Reader

A posteriori to Axiom

No.	Term	Definition
1.	A posteriori	Latin term meaning *based on evidence or experience*. Thus, an a posteriori statement is normally based on some empirical type evidence rather than on an assumption only.
2.	A priori	Latin term meaning *from the beginning*. Usually used when referring to axioms which are not questioned. It may also be used when describing the underlying assumptions of the research. In academic research there are always a priori assumptions, and these should be kept to a minimum. Descartes' a priori truth is *I think, therefore I am*.
3.	Ab initio	Latin term meaning *from the beginning*.
4.	Abduction	A word suggested by Charles Saunders Pierce who was one of the founding members of the American Pragmatist school of thought in the 19th Century. The term is now seldom used as much more emphasis is placed on deduction and induction. It is a

Glossary of Research Concepts and Issues

No.	Term	Definition
		method of inference, sometimes called a methodology of discovery with a connection to induction. It has some similarities to induction, but it uses a level of intuition which is sometimes described as having a "hunch".
		Those researchers using abduction will have no hesitation in guessing what the outcome of a research activity might be and then initiating some sort of procedure to test their guess.
		http://jigpal.oxfordjournals.org/cgi/content/abstract/14/2/179
5.	Abeyance	Research degree candidates sometimes find it useful to have a pause from their research. This may come about due to pressure at work, health problems or family circumstances. The term abeyance is used by some universities when the research project is paused. During abeyance the requirement to pay fees is normally suspended and the period of the abeyance is not counted against the degree.
		Many universities are prepared to offer one abeyance period of up to a year to a degree candidate without much formal justification.
		See *Off books*
6.	Abstract	In academic research an abstract is a short summary of the research which is usually placed at the beginning of the research report or the dissertation or the paper. It should briefly address all the important

Glossary of Research Concepts and Issues

No.	Term	Definition
		aspects of the research. An abstract is a document of considerable importance as many researchers will decide on whether or not to read the main report or paper on the basis of the abstract. Despite this, abstracts are often poorly and carelessly written.
7.	Abstracting service	A service which provides abstracts of published academic papers enabling researchers to quickly identify if a paper is likely to be of value to their research. These are usually paid for services.
8.	Abstraction	The expression of concepts and processes in such a way that the ideas could be applicable to different circumstances and situations. The creation of abstractions from particular observations is a key characteristic of academic research findings. Creating abstractions is the first step in developing a theory.
9.	Academic expression	Academic expression can refer to the verbal and written way in which academic research is described. See *Academic Writing*
10.	Academic research	The process of adding something of value to the body of theoretical and practical knowledge in response to a question or questions. In addition, an important characteristic of academic research is that it needs to be presented in such a way as to

Glossary of Research Concepts and Issues

No.	Term	Definition
		demonstrate a high degree of scholarship on the part of the researcher.
11.	Academic writing	Academic writing is different to report writing. It should not be taken for granted that a novice to academic research will be able to write adequately. Academic writing needs to be formal, but not pretentious. It is important that the research is described in moderate language with minimal use of adjectives and adverbs such as *very* and *wonderfully* or *incredibly*. There should be as little ambiguity as possible. Words without clear definitions such as *abundance, plethora, dearth* etc., should be avoided. Academic writing is a learned skill which takes time and concentration to acquire.
12.	Academic attire/dress	Traditionally academic dress consists of a gown, short for undergraduates and long for post graduates, a hood and a piece of head wear. A flat-topped cap with a tassel referred to as a mortar board is often, but not exclusively used. The colours of the gown, hood and headwear vary from university to university and from faculty to faculty within the same institution. Individuals holding high office within the university often wear much more elaborate gowns etc.
13.	Academic judgement	Academic research needs to be assessed or evaluated. There are no fixed and immutable rules as to how this should be done. Nor is there a clear set of standards which may

Glossary of Research Concepts and Issues

No.	Term	Definition
		easily be referenced. Experienced academic opinion using what is loosely referred to as academic judgement is the approach which is used. The judgements of academics can conflict with one another.
14.	Access	It is sometimes said that gaining access to those with appropriate data is one of the most challenging aspects of academic research. Access implies a range of activities such as interviews, conversations, written material, individuals who complete questionnaires, among others. Access is hardly ever easy, and a lack of access can sometimes prevent a research project from proceeding. It is sometimes a great disappointment to academic researchers that not everyone is interested in sharing their insights with the research community. Access to appropriate informants should never be taken for granted.
15.	Acknowledgements	In general, it is regarded as a common courtesy for a researcher to acknowledge the assistance provided by his or her supervisor/s and others who have gone out of their way to assist during the course of the research.
16.	Action learning	Learning and research are sometimes thought to be similar if not the same activity. If this is the case, then action learning and action research are tightly coupled concepts. The root of this idea is that we learn by

Glossary of Research Concepts and Issues

No.	Term	Definition
		doing and that the roots of research are often in some form of doing.
		Action learning has been described as a form of research in which the researcher becomes involved in undertaking work with those individuals who are being researched, or who are working for the organisation being researched.
17.	Action research	An approach to conducting research whereby the researcher leads a project in a host organisation and has the authority to design and implement the project in such a way that he/she may either test a set of theoretical conjectures or a set of hypotheses, or alternatively acquire data for the purpose of theory development. The researcher is responsible for the success of the project.
		Action research presents several challenges concerning obtaining access to an organisation and thus it is normally only used by part time researchers who can obtain the cooperation of their employer.
		Action research also requires the researcher to lead a group of employees who evaluate the success of the intervention and by implication also evaluate the researcher's skill in managing the project.
18.	Ad absurdum (reductio)	Latin term meaning *to absurdity*. It is a term which describes a manner of arguing which follows an approach which leads to an absurd position. Reductio ad absurdum refers

6

Glossary of Research Concepts and Issues

No.	Term	Definition
		to taking an argument to a point where it is clearly nonsense and its absurdity will be recognised by those involved with the argument.
		This type of argument takes the following form. It is said that drinking copious volumes of water is good for bodily functions. If this is so then it might be argued that one should drink as much water as one possibly can. However, it is possible to upset the chemical balance of the body by drinking too much water. Therefore, drinking copious volumes of water is not good for bodily functions.
19.	Ad hoc	Latin term meaning *for this purpose*. In research this refers to something which is undertaken without any formal planning such as: We had an ad hoc meeting with the ethics committee to discuss the questionnaire.
20.	Ad infinitum	Latin term normally used to mean *to continue forever without stopping*. This is of course nearly always an exaggeration, except perhaps when it is said that the universe stretches on and on ad infinitum.
21.	Agnostic	In the research philosophy context being agnostic means professing a claim that it is not possible to have any certain knowledge. But in general research terms it is used differently such as, "I am agnostic as to whether my doctoral degree candidates are positivists or interpretivists". In normal English

Glossary of Research Concepts and Issues

No.	Term	Definition
		usage the term is usually used in connection with a non-belief in a deity.
22.	Alternative hypothesis	Hypothesis testing attempts to reject a claim which is made by the researcher.
		For example, the claim could be in the form "marketing managers have greater influence on corporate strategy than production managers".
		The claim is referred to by researchers as the null hypothesis. If this claim is rejected, then the alternative hypothesis which needs to be stated at the same time as the null hypothesis is accepted (pro tem).
		The method of testing will vary depending on the type of data to which the researcher has access.
23.	Ambiguity	An expression or a piece of text can be regarded as having more than one meaning. Furthermore, it is not always clear which meaning the speaker or the author intends to convey. The researcher needs to be able to identify ambiguity and to ensure that he or she understands the meaning which was intended to be conveyed. It is also important to minimise if not complete avoid any ambiguity in the research dissertation.
24.	American pragmatism	See *Pragmatism*

Glossary of Research Concepts and Issues

No.	Term	Definition
25.	Analysis	Analysis is always performed on data and conducted with a question in mind. The analysis of an object or a phenomenon requires that it is closely inspected in order to establish its nature and its content. Analysis will explore the object or the phenomenon beyond its obvious or superficial appearance. In so doing it may be appropriate to take a holistic view and focus on the object or phenomenon within its context. On the other hand, it is sometime more effective to take a reductionist stance and analyse the details of various dimensions or components of the object or phenomenon. Sometimes both approaches may be conducted simultaneously.
26.	Analytical induction	A term which emphasises the nature of the research process which requires a focus on events and the detailed study of their connections and consequences.
27.	Andragogy	Education aimed at adults. This subject discusses how to engage adults and the processes involved in their learning.
28.	Androcentricity	Approaching research from a male gender perspective and taking the view that issues relating to males and their interests are primary.
29.	Annotated bibliography	A list of relevant and appropriate published sources of information compiled by the researcher which has been produced together with some level of review or evaluation. Creating an annotated bibliography is sometime

Glossary of Research Concepts and Issues

No.	Term	Definition
		regarded as the first step in any substantial academic research project.
		Developing an annotated bibliography is a major undertaking.
30.	Anonymity	Academic researchers are expected to protect the identity of their informants to prevent unfortunate consequences for the informant participating in the research project. Ethics protocols often state that the source of the evidence will be anonymised as soon as possible.
		Sometimes it can be challenging if not actually impossible to anonymise a source of evidence as the type of data acquired could only come from one person or a small number of individuals which could be traced.
31.	Anthology	A group of writings published as a compilation of different works normally in book form for easy reference.
32.	Anthropomorphism	Assigning human characteristics to animals or other non-human entities or objects.
33.	Anti-plagiarism software	A computer program which checks text to determine if it is original work or whether it contains text which has already appeared in other published work.
34.	Anti-positivism	A rejection of the principles of positivism and a preference for an interpretivist approach to research. Anti-positivism is a negative term which is sometimes used disparagingly to describe those who are arguing for a

No.	Term	Definition
		different interpretivist and perhaps qualitative way of conducting academic research.
35.	Antithesis	The opposite of thesis. It is a term used in the description of the dialectic to explain how an argument evolves towards a clearer understanding among those who are engaged in a discussion.
36.	Anything goes	A term used by Paul Feyerabend to suggest that there is no privileged path (or intellectual high road) to the creation of knowledge. A researcher may use any approach which will be accepted by his/her community. In academic research this means the research needs to be acceptable to the examiners or reviewers as well as to editors of academic journals. Anything goes does not imply low standards of rigor.
37.	Appeals	In some circumstances research degree candidates may disagree with how the rules of the institution are being interpreted and applied to their work. This disagreement may involve the results of the examination of a dissertation. When this happens a research degree candidate can appeal against the decision of the examiners. Universities have strict rules about how the appeal process functions and in general appeals cannot be made against academic judgement of the examiners. This means that appeals would have to be addressed to

Glossary of Research Concepts and Issues

No.	Term	Definition
		problems with the processes associated with the candidate's degree experience.
38.	Applied research	Application orientated research. Sometimes business and management consulting work is described as applied research. In such cases this type of research may not have much academic value.
39.	Appointing examiners	Examiners (normally at least two and sometimes three) need to be appointed to evaluate research degree submissions i.e. dissertations or theses. Examiners should be both competent in the field of study as well as being comfortable with the research methodology used by the degree candidate. It is the university's responsibility to find appropriate examiners for a research degree candidate.
40.	Appreciative enquiry	A model of analysis of decision making and research in organisations which was developed in the late 1980s. It is based on an analysis of the best aspects of any situation in order to image what could be achieved.
41.	Aptitude	An aptitude is a natural ability. In the case of academic research, the primary aptitude required is normally considered to be scholarship. See *Scholarship*
42.	Archiving	The recording and maintenance of documents for future reference. When documents are archived they are taken out of

Glossary of Research Concepts and Issues

No.	Term	Definition
		general circulation and stored securely under the control of an archivist.
43.	Arguing evidentially	An argument based on specific evidence or data acquired by the researcher.
44.	Arguing from authority or logically	Arguments based on established authority (normally in the form of the published work of well-established academic leaders in the field) or by the use of logic-based inference often related to such authority.
45.	Argument	A series of logical statements leading to a convincing conclusion. Arguments are a key aspect of academic research whether it is theoretical or empirical, positivist or interpretivist. The quality of academic research is often judged on the strength of the argument underpinning the findings and therefore argument is a central issue in academic research.
46.	Artificial intelligence	The idea that it will be possible to create an entity either in software or a machine which will be able to display intellectual behaviour which will be indistinguishable from that of a human being. To date although progress in this respect has been considerable in that computer systems can play chess as well as the best humans and they can win quiz competitions, there is still much to be done. The concept of artificial intelligence was originally suggested in the theory of computation by Alan Turning and has been

Glossary of Research Concepts and Issues

No.	Term	Definition
		developed into an academic field of study since the 1950s. The main difficulty encountered by this field of study has been the definition or even the description of natural intelligence.
47.	Assumptions	Academic research is based on a series of assumptions. Perhaps the most basic assumption is that the research question is answerable, although there is an argument that more fundamental than this is the assumption that an answer to the question would be of value to anyone.
		On a less philosophical level there are always assumptions about the availability of data. Assumptions underpin the researcher's belief in the integrity of the data as well as the most appropriate ways to acquire it, manage it, analyse it and interpret it.
48.	Asymmetrical interviews	In the context of research interviews the term asymmetrical refers to when there is not a balance between the information supplied by the researcher and by the knowledgeable informant.
		In one sense or another many interviews are asymmetrical. It could be argued that interviews should be asymmetrical as an interview is an evidence collection event which needs to make available information to the researcher and not vice versa.
		See *Miner metaphor*

Glossary of Research Concepts and Issues

No.	Term	Definition
49.	ATLAS/ti	Software package which provides tools to facilitate qualitative data coding, storage and retrieval. It also has facilities for perceptual mapping to support theoretical conjecture development
50.	Attitude scale	An instrument for measuring attitudes often but not always using a questionnaire and using ordinal data.
51.	Attribution theory	A theory which describes how individuals perceive or ascribe causes to other individuals or events or particular phenomena.
52.	Attrition	The rate at which individuals drop out of a research study.
53.	Audit trail	A term borrowed from the accounting profession. An audit trail in the research context is a record of the events which took place during the research process and how the researcher perceived them. It should describe how the thinking of the researcher evolved over the period of the research.
54.	Authenticity	Something is said to be authentic if it is a fair representation of that which it purports to be and there is no hidden agenda associated with it. For the credibility of qualitative research to be recognized it is important that the informants are perceived to be able to deliver authentic accounts of their experiences.

Glossary of Research Concepts and Issues

No.	Term	Definition
55.	Author date referencing system	See *Harvard Referencing System* which uses the author's name/s and date of publication as the reference data.
56.	Author/s	The named individuals who have researched and/or written the book or academic publication. In most academic communities the number of authors whose name may be associated with a piece of work will be limited to a handful of people. However medical research can have hundreds of authors on one single paper.
57.	Auto ethnography	A narrative account written in a reflexive manner which relates the detailed experiences of the researcher to the wider context of his or her environment. It is a relatively new approach to academic research which at present would only be accepted by a small community of scholars.
58.	Auto-writers	Software products which claim to be able to write essays for students and papers for academics.
59.	Awarding a research degree	A research degree is normally awarded if both the external and internal examiners agree that the dissertation has achieved the required standard. In the case of a doctorate, it is also often necessary that the degree candidate has successfully presented his or her ideas at an oral examination. The degree is usually awarded by the University Senate

No.	Term	Definition
		on the recommendation of a Higher Degrees Committee.
60.	Axial coding	A term associated with Grounded Theory Method referring to a second order level of coding using open codes as its raw material. This involves grouping open codes (first level codes) to constitute more comprehensive constructs leading to a fuller understanding of the text.
61.	Axiom	A proposition which is considered to be self-evident and/or be true by definition. Axioms are established a priori and accepted at the outset of the discussion. In formal subjects such as mathematics and logic axioms underpin any form of "proof". In most western cultures it is axiomatic that knowledge is a good thing. http://www.answers.com/topic/axiom

Glossary of Research Concepts and Issues

Basic Research to Bursary

No.	Term	Definition
62.	Basic research	Research which addresses questions, the answers to which may not be of immediate practical value. The term fundamental research is also sometimes used to describe this level of research. This type of research is not normally conducted in the social sciences but rather in the physical or life sciences.
63.	Best fit	In seeking to find a pattern in a scatter diagram, researchers will often attempt to produce a mathematical equation which represents the "best fit" line that could be used to describe the relationship between the variables being studied. See *Scatter diagram*
64.	Bias	The term bias is used in a number of different senses in academic research and may refer to the introduction of a non-random element in the choices made by the researcher. From a statistical point

No.	Term	Definition
		of view bias refers to systematic error which could be due to the choice of sample, measurement technique or some other element of research design. Bias may also be introduced during the analysis, interpretation and conclusion phases of the research. A bias may be the result of a preconception of the characteristics of a person, a situation or an organization, to mention only three sources of bias. It can be difficult for a researcher to be aware of his or her biases.
		In a more general sense bias may be introduced due to a range of research preferences including the types of organisation the researcher wishes to study, as well as the level of individuals who are sought as informants and the amount of attention which particular informants receive from a researcher.
		Bias is ubiquitous in academic research and the researcher needs to try to be aware of his or her biases and minimize their impact on his or her research.
65.	Bibliography	A list of published texts (including websites and videos) known to the researcher which are of relevance to the research topic. Sometimes a few non-published sources can be included. The word bibliography is not a synonym for the term Reference List.

Glossary of Research Concepts and Issues

No.	Term	Definition
66.	Bibliometrics	The application of mathematics and statistics to the understanding of patterns in the publication of ideas and concepts in academics papers and books.
67.	Big data	A term used in different ways, one of which is the employment of large data sets together with data mining techniques. This is sometimes referred to as data-led research. An increasingly common application of big data is sentiment analysis.
68.	Black hole of philosophy	Academic research in general, and at doctoral level in particular, will have a particular philosophical underpinning which will be reflected in the ontological and epistemological assumptions which the researcher makes. It is important that the researcher understands these issues. However, they can be complex, and some researchers will spend more time than is necessary addressing philosophy rather than the more practical process of research. When this happens, it becomes a problem and has been referred to as falling into the black hole of philosophy.
69.	Blind reviewing and double blind reviewing	In a blind review situation, the reviewer does not know who the author of the work being reviewed is, or vice versa. When both the author and reviewer are unknown to each other, this reviewing arrangement is referred to as double

Glossary of Research Concepts and Issues

No.	Term	Definition
		blind reviewing. Note that double blind reviewing does not mean that the work is reviewed twice i.e. by two reviewers.
70.	Blog	The word blog is a combination of the words web and log. It is a means of recording thoughts on the internet which it is hoped will lead to a conversation or exchange of ideas with others interested in the same topic.
71.	Bloggers code of conduct	Inappropriate words and comments can appear on blogs and it is the responsibility of the creator of the blog to ensure that these are removed. http://en.wikipedia.org/wiki/Blogger's_Code_of_Conduct
72.	Body of knowledge	In academic research the body of knowledge is the set of concepts, theories, models and other elements of knowledge which are accepted by the community interested in the topic concerned. The issue of acceptance by the community is important. For example, some individuals might not regard homeopathy as being part of the body of knowledge of medical science.
73.	Bursary	Money which is made available to support students in their study. A bursary may be a small amount of money or it could be substantial funding. Bursaries are sometimes awarded on the grounds of past academic excellence but not always. There is sometimes considerable

No.	Term	Definition
		overlap between scholarships and bursaries. Unlike a grant the money obtained from a bursary is not normally refundable, although sometimes a bursary comes with a condition related to future employment with the donor. See *Scholarship - Money*

Glossary of Research Concepts and Issues

Capacity to consent to Cum Laude

No.	Term	Definition
74.	Capacity to consent	Data should not be acquired from informants who have not provided their consent in writing. This is generally in the form of a signed letter of consent. However not everyone may be regarded as being able to give their informed consent. An individual's capacity to consent may be affected by his or her medical condition or by other circumstances. For example, if individuals are asked to participate in a research project being conducted by their immediate boss. Similarly, children would generally not be regarded as having an independent capacity to consent without the agreement/endorsement of their parents.
75.	Case history	A term sometimes used as a synonym for a case study, but which will typically have a teaching or learning orientation rather than being an instrument for academic research.

Glossary of Research Concepts and Issues

No.	Term	Definition
76.	Case study or case study research	An umbrella term which refers to a selection of data collection and analysis approaches which are used to understand a particular instance of a phenomenon. A case study should be a contemporary investigation where the boundaries between the phenomenon and its context are not clearly evident or may be interpreted differently by different researchers. A case study will use multiple sources of evidence. Case study research will rely heavily on qualitative data but may include some quantitative data and even some quantitative analytical techniques. A case study will always be reported in the form of a narrative. http://www.experiment-resources.com/case-study-research-design.html
77.	Case study teaching	In this context a case study is a story or a scenario which is offered to the student/s for the purposes of stimulating a discussion from which learning will take place. Case study teaching has become a popular pedagogical principle in a number of different faculties especially business schools. Its success can be attributed to Harvard Business School where it is the primary modus operandi.

Glossary of Research Concepts and Issues

No.	Term	Definition
		There is no reason why a teaching-learning case study needs to be factual. An imagined scenario may be the most effective way to draw the student's attention to all the points required by the syllabus.
78.	Cash value	A term coined by the American Pragmatists which focuses on the need for research findings to have a practical and useful outcome for society. Some academics would consider this term rather crass.
79.	CASIC	Computer Assisted Survey Information Collection. One of a number of tools which facilitate the collection of data for the purposes of research.
80.	Category	A Grounded Theory Method term approximating a variable or a concept or a construct. In the Grounded Theory Method data is collected, examined, coded and reflected upon in order to establish categories as a step towards developing a theory.
81.	Causal inference	When examining a data set representing two or more variables it is sometimes suggested that a change in some variables causes a resulting change in others. Positing such a relationship is referred to as suggesting a causal inference.

Glossary of Research Concepts and Issues

No.	Term	Definition
		See *Cause and effect*
82.	Cause and effect	Two or more variables are said to be in a relationship of cause and effect if the occurrence of a change in the first variable causes a change in the second variable. The causal variable (i.e. the independent variable) has to be in temporal priority to the effect variable (i.e. dependent variable) and there has to be evidence and a clear logical reason to assert that there is such a relationship between the variables. Cause and effect should not be confused with association where the variables may change together but the independent variable does not cause the change to occur.
83.	Census	When it is possible to record and include all the data points in a population, then it is said that a census has been conducted.
84.	Central tendency	A term used to give some meaning to the concept of an average. The central tendency can be understood as the typical value of a data set or it could be expressed as that value from which the next data element in the data set is likely to have the least deviation.
85.	Certificate of own work	Research dissertations require the author to certify that the work undertaken was conducted by the researcher. This

No.	Term	Definition
		certificate is included in the leading pages of the dissertation. Of course, some minor tasks may have been outsourced.
		See *Outsourced*
86.	Certifications	Universities require a number of assurances which need to be given by the research degree candidates when a dissertation is submitted for examination. These are presented in the form of certificates which include the certificate of own work, a certificate that the researcher has not presented the same work to another university for another degree, a certificate that the work may be included in the university library.
87.	Ceteris paribus	Latin term meaning *all other things being equal* which may be translated into nothing else changes. This is an important assumption for all research. Except for certain limited situations which may be reproduced in a laboratory, scientific research is often faced with too many variables to control. In such situations the variables which are not controlled are effectively ignored. The variables not under the control of the researcher are assumed not to change i.e. the rule of ceteris paribus is applied.
		An example of this in Economics is the Law of Demand. The Law of Demand states, ceteris paribus, the quantity

Glossary of Research Concepts and Issues

No.	Term	Definition
		demanded is a function of the price of the product or service. The ceteris paribus assumption allows government policy, competitive activity, consumer taste, advertising expenditure and other factors to be ignored.
88.	Changing supervisors	One or more supervisors are normally allocated to a research degree candidate shortly after registration has been completed. This is sometimes done without appropriate consideration as to whether the supervisor/s and the degree candidates will be able to work well together.
		If the relationship between these individuals does not work, then the degree candidate may request a change of supervisor/s. This should not be undertaken lightly.
89.	Chatham House Rule	If a meeting is held under the Chatham House Rule then the participants are free to use any information which they acquire during the meeting but they agree that they will not disclose the source of any specific remarks made by any individual.
90.	Cheating	An activity in which a researcher breaks any aspect of the moral code applicable to academic research. One of the most common forms of cheating is plagiarism although it is by no means the only one. Lying about how many interviews were

Glossary of Research Concepts and Issues

No.	Term	Definition
		conducted and what data was acquired is another form of cheating. Cheating involves acquiring an unfair advantage at the expense of others who are competing for the same degree of academic honour and is thus regarded as unfair and not acceptable behaviour. It is regularly claimed that cheating is on the increase and this assertion is supported by the number of websites offering student assistance including writing essays, reports and dissertations on their behalf, which many universities would consider questionable if not outright cheating. See *Professor Sir Cyril Burt* http://web.stanford.edu/class/engr110/cheating.html http://policies.uws.edu.au/view.current.php?id=00051
91.	Cherry picking research	Selecting data carefully to support a hypothesis or several hypotheses.
92.	Child/Children orientated research	Special ethics clearance is normally required when an academic research project involves the participation of children. Children may not have the capacity to provide informed consent and their parents and teachers may need to consent as well. In some circumstances police clearance may also be needed.

Glossary of Research Concepts and Issues

No.	Term	Definition
93.	Chronology	A study focusing on events occurring over time. A chronology is sometimes described as a time line and lays out a situation which is discussed in terms of timings (often the dates) at which certain events occurred. http://www.merriam-webster.com/dictionary/chronology
94.	Citation	When a paper is referenced in the work of another author in either a book or another paper the original author is said to have been cited by the latter.
95.	Citation management software	Used to establish your own database of references. http://www.unisa.edu.au/ltu/students/study/referencing/harvard.pdf
96.	Citation analysis	The investigation of the frequency and the location of citations related to either an author or a publication. It may employ a range of metrics such as the G-Index or the H-Index.
97.	Citation index	A measure of the frequency with which an author is referenced or cited by other researchers in their published work. The website www.Harzing.com offers some information on citation indices for academic researchers.
98.	Citation tail	Citations in scholarly papers are known to have heavy tail distributions which results in there being some elements

No.	Term	Definition
		quite far from the mean. This suggests that the population is not strictly normal but skewed.
99.	Clockwork world/universe	The belief which is now to a large extent discredited that the physical world is controlled by a series of laws similar to those on which a time piece is based, which determine all aspects of the world/universe.
100.	Closed question	A question used in a questionnaire to which there is a limited choice of answers such as Do you smoke? Yes or No.
101.	Cloud	A reference to computers operating through the internet and thus making software and data available to researchers from many different locations. The user is said to be connected to the software and the data through the cloud.
102.	Code consolidating	Sometimes when organising data too many codes have been used and it is necessary to group certain codes under a new supra-code or heading.
103.	Code splitting	During a coding exercise it may become apparent that the allocated codes do not produce the requited degree of granularity. If this happens then new codes may be established and items which were originally coded under one heading may be split up over the new codes thus created.

Glossary of Research Concepts and Issues

No.	Term	Definition
104.	Codes	The use of numeric or alphabetic characters to designate and group data or ideas as part of the process of data analysis and understanding. The identification of the codes to use is an important part of the analysis, interpretation and understanding processes of research. The importance of the selection and management of the codes is often an under emphasised issue.
105.	Cognitive capacity	Cognitive capacity refers to the ability to observe, analyse, combine, and synthesise ideas. It also embraces the notion of our ability to understand and to express our understanding.
106.	Collaborative-participative research	This concept is mostly used in action research to describe the relationship between the researcher and the individuals in the organization in which the action research is being conducted.
107.	Collegiality	The notion of collegiality is rooted in the view that academics are part of a community of scholars and that there should be a relationship of collaboration based on mutual respect among colleagues in a university or other scholarly setting.
108.	Colloquium	An event at which research degree candidates present their work and are

Glossary of Research Concepts and Issues

No.	Term	Definition
		offered feedback by experienced researchers.
		Presenting at a colloquium has become an integral part of most research degree programmes.
109.	Commencement	A term used by some universities in place of graduation. It is an old-fashioned way of describing the status of a university graduate. When a person has been through the commencement ceremony, he or she may now commence their contribution to the discourse of the university.
		See *Graduations*
110.	Commitment	The desire of the degree candidate to obtain the degree which is converted into effort.
111.	Complaints	Degree candidates are increasingly critical of the level of service they receive from universities. These criticisms sometimes lead to complaints and in turn complaints have resulted in court cases.
112.	Completion rate	The percentage of research participants who complete a task such as answering a questionnaire.
		This term is also used to refer to the percentage of research degree candidates who finish their degree

Glossary of Research Concepts and Issues

No.	Term	Definition
		programmes and are awarded their degrees.
113.	Computer Assisted Qualitative Data Analysis (CAQDAS).	Software which may assist a researcher in obtaining a greater understanding of qualitative data. The software requires the data to be coded and the program then allows the researcher to perform rapid sorting and cross tabulation activities which may help develop a more comprehensive understanding of the data. http://www.restore.ac.uk/lboro/research/software/caqdas_comparison.php
114.	Computer aided interviewing	A system whereby an informant answers a questionnaire on a computer screen. http://ukdataservice.ac.uk/media/262820/discover_caifactsheet.pdf
115.	Concept mapping	An approach to data analysis where different concepts or constructs are visually represented on a graph which shows the relative position of other concepts or constructs. This allows the researcher to seek commonality and differences between ideas and their sources, for example. Concept mapping is often performed using specialized computer software.

Glossary of Research Concepts and Issues

No.	Term	Definition
116.	Conclusions	Research findings on their own will generally not provide the degree of insight sought by an academic researcher. Thus, the researcher needs to summarise the findings and to state what they mean to his/her community. This part of the research is referred to as writing or producing the conclusions and is a key part of any academic research project in the social sciences. Increasingly researchers are expected to state what they regard as the implications of their conclusions.
117.	Confidentiality	Researchers are expected to offer confidentiality and to ensure that data/evidence supplied by knowledgeable informants is not disseminated to anyone else and that where possible the data is anonymised. It is important that this promise of confidentiality is honoured wherever possible by the researcher. If certain criminal activities were to be encountered during the research the research may be obliged to inform the authorities.
118.	Confirmation bias	Refers to a tendency for the researcher to look for data which will confirm his/her values, concerns or preconceptions and to avoid data which may contradict the preconceptions. This bias will impact on all aspects of the research including how a particular data set is

Glossary of Research Concepts and Issues

No.	Term	Definition
		interpreted and what this interpretation might mean.
119.	Confounding variables	In statistics a confounding variable is an extraneous variable which correlates with the dependent or independent variable/s and which causes the model which has been developed to mislead the researcher. A confounding variable can lead to a fatal flaw in the research outcome.
120.	Consilience	Refers to a situation in which there are multiple sources of evidence supporting a proposition. In this case these different forms or sources of evidence are said to converge independently.
121.	Consistency	There is a need to take the same approach when working with different informants and in the handling of data collected there from. Any differences can make the comparison of data problematic. In academic research inconsistency can produce invalid results.
122.	Constant comparative method	A term used mostly in the Grounded Theory Method which refers to the need for the researcher to be continually aware of how data being collected may relate to other data previously found.
		The meaning of data is often most clearly understood when it is compared to another data set and this is the

Glossary of Research Concepts and Issues

No.	Term	Definition
		motivation for the idea of Constant comparison.
123.	Constant comparative analysis	This refers to a research approach whereby the emphasis is on seeking similarities and differences between the participants examined during the research. Constant comparative analysis is a fundamental driver of the Grounded Theory Method.
124.	Construct	A construct is a complex idea or concept which normally embraces more than one aspect of the matter/subject being studied, i.e. it is not a simple variable. For example leadership may be seen as a construct and leadership involves the ability to inspire people, to motivate them, to influence them and to offer them some sort of satisfaction for following the leader's proposed course of action.
125.	Construct validity	Construct validity requires the researcher to satisfy him/herself that the operationalised variables may confidently be regarded to be part of the construct being investigated and to what extent it can be generalised. http://writing.colostate.edu/guides/research/relval/com2b5.cfm
126.	Constructionism	The terms constructionism, social constructionism and constructivism are often used interchangeably in social

Glossary of Research Concepts and Issues

No.	Term	Definition
		science research. Some researchers object to this, asserting that they are quite different. Anyone wanting to be in command of this topic needs to explore these arguments in detail. There are a number of explanations of what constitutes constructionism.
		Constructionism can be seen as a response to essentialism. A constructionist argues that we do not live in one objective reality which is independent of our minds. He/she will argue that what an individual observes is influenced by how he/she constructs his/her view of the world. This means that any given situation will be understood in different ways by different people. Constructionism can be contrasted with realism which asserts that the world is independent of the minds of individuals who try to understand it.
		http://www.psy.dmu.ac.uk/michael/soc_con_disc.htm
127.	Constructivism	See *Social constructivism*
128.	Contemporary literature	In a literature review more recent publications are generally more interesting than older publications unless the older publications are seminal in the field of study. The period for which literature may be considered contemporary varies from topic to topic, but papers older

Glossary of Research Concepts and Issues

No.	Term	Definition
		than 10 or maybe even 5 years may not be considered contemporary.
129.	Content analysis	A technique used by researchers to acquire a richer understanding of data supplied by knowledge informants. This technique involves identifying the major concepts or issues discussed in an interview for example and then the counting of the number of occurrences of these concepts or issues. Content analysis may also be performed on text such as that obtained from published papers, internal reports or archives.
130.	Content validity	Content validity is demonstrated by the degree to which specific questions, in a questionnaire or in an interview schedule, maps or corresponds to the research questions/hypotheses.
131.	Contingency theory	Refers to theories in behavioural science which point out that there is no privileged way of understanding a situation other than by looking at the environment and seeing what factors directly affect the situation at that time. This emphasises the fact that social science deals with people and organisations which are directly affected by the circumstances in which they are found.
132.	Contradictory results	When mixed methods are employed it is possible that the analysis of different data sources can result in contradictory results. If this situation arises it is

Glossary of Research Concepts and Issues

No.	Term	Definition
		necessary for the researcher to be able to offer a satisfactory explanation as to why this has occurred.
133.	Contribution	The objective of academic research is to make a contribution to the body of theoretical and practical knowledge. The term contribution is used to describe that which has been added to the body of theoretical knowledge by the academic research.
		It can be challenging to identify a particular contribution and there can be differences in opinion about whether a contribution has actually been made.
134.	Control group	In experimental research it is sometimes necessary to consider two or more groups of research participants. One group is subjected to the experiment intervention and the other group is not. The group which is not subjected to the experiment intervention is referred to as the control group. In such a case the main purpose of the experiment is to understand how the outcome of intervention has affected the non-control group relative to the control group.
135.	Convenience sample	The use of a group of people to supply data who are accessed because it is easy to do so. An example of this is a classroom of students who are asked to complete a questionnaire in order to

Glossary of Research Concepts and Issues

No.	Term	Definition
		facilitate the lecturer's research. A convenience sample has a low status in academic research.
136.	Conversation analysis	The study of human interactions of both the verbal and non-verbal variety. It is to some extent associated with Ethno-methodology.
137.	Copy editing	A more detailed and thorough form of proof reading (See *Proof reading*). A copy editor would tend to have some understanding of the subject matter as well as the rules of syntax.
138.	Copyright and trademarks	If product names are used in a dissertation it is good practice to acknowledge who is the owner of any copyright or trademarks associated with these.
139.	Corrections (to dissertations)	See *Revisions*
140.	Correlation	A measure of the relationship between two or more variables. The fact that there is a numeric relationship between the variable does not mean that there is any cause-and-effect mechanism connecting the variables.
141.	Correspondence analysis	Correspondence analysis is sometimes described as an extension of content analysis as it requires data similar to content analysis. However correspondence analysis requires the creation of a 2 by 2 matrix which records the major concepts or issues discussed. It also

Glossary of Research Concepts and Issues

No.	Term	Definition
		reflects who mentioned which concepts or issues. With this matrix it is possible to produce a number of reports which show the association of the concepts or issues and the different groups which held these views. Note that in this context the word Correspondence is from the French word meaning association or connection and should not be confused with the notion of writing.
142.	Corroboration	Finding data or evidence which will support other information obtained or which will give further credence to a theory being developed. It is sometimes suggested, incorrectly, that the prime purpose of triangulations is corroboration.
143.	Cost-benefit analysis	An examination of the costs of a project which are then compared to benefits perceived or indeed realised.
144.	Covert observation	This involves researchers conducting the research project on a surreptitious basis. This suggests that an ethics protocol has probably not been approved by the university, as obtaining informed consent from anyone who is involved is now normally a prerequisite.
145.	Creativity	An essential element in academic research which may be described as the ability to look at a situation and to perceive how it could be accounted for in a

Glossary of Research Concepts and Issues

No.	Term	Definition
		different way than has been done before.
146.	Credibility	A characteristic of research which allows it to be believed and thus gives it value to the academic community. It may be seen as the qualitative research equivalent of validity.
147.	Criminal reporting	Researchers sometimes encounter criminal activity by individuals or organisations whom they are researching. Whether or not it is necessary to report these to the authorities depends upon the exact circumstances. However, if money laundering or terrorist activity is suspected the researcher is required to report this.
148.	Critical realism	An approach to research which is firmly based in a realist as opposed to a constructivist understanding of the world. Critical realists are agnostic with regards to the positivists-interpretivist debate. In fact, critical realists often welcome an approach which resembles a mixed methods strategy which incorporates quantitative and qualitative data. It considers both positivism and social constructivism too superficial in their approach to the creation of knowledge. The term critical realism is used by different researchers in different ways depending on their background. Underpinning critical realism is the realisation

Glossary of Research Concepts and Issues

No.	Term	Definition
		that it is necessary to be critical of what we observe (in the sense of the way the term critical is used in critical theory) and that realism can be confused with representationalism which should be avoided. Critical realists will try to transcend the space between the established traditions of the physical and life sciences and the traditions of the social sciences.
		This is a specialist approach to research which has a relatively small following. Roy Bhaskar is regarded as one of the leading thinkers in this field. http://www.criticalrealism.de-mon.co.uk/#about
149.	Critical success factors	Critical success factors are those factors or issues which have to be present for a project to succeed. The critical success factors for a research degree are regarded as being commitment, management and aptitude. These are not stated in order of importance. The order of importance will depend upon the individual.
150.	Critical theory	The term critical theory usually denotes a specialised approach to research firmly based in the thinking of the Frankfurt School which was founded in the aftermath of the WW1. In its original form critical theory was perceived to have a degree of Marxist underpinning.

Glossary of Research Concepts and Issues

No.	Term	Definition
		It is not a main stream approach to academic research.
		Critical theorists believe that science is not value free and critical theory is believed by its practitioners to be orientated towards real practical issues with an agenda to liberate or emancipate those who are the subject of the research. Critical theory challenges assumptions which other research and researchers might not. Critical theory tends to acknowledge the difficulty of conducting unbiased research and therefore requires the admission of the researchers' prejudices.
		This is a controversial approach to research.
		http://plato.stanford.edu/entries/critical-theory/
		http://www.youtube.com/watch?v=5ULLZm_x_YE
		http://www.youtube.com/watch?v=5ULLZm_x_YE
151.	Critique	Reviewing a piece of work pointing out both its strengths and weaknesses and usually drawing a conclusion as to whether the work has overall merit or not. This process is sometimes referred to as critical reflection or writing a critique.

Glossary of Research Concepts and Issues

No.	Term	Definition
152.	Cross case analysis	When a research study involves a number of different case studies it is useful to compare the findings in one case study with the findings in other case studies. This is referred to as cross case analysis.
153.	Cross sectional research	Cross sectional research contrasts with longitudinal research. Cross sectional research considers an organisation, a person, a country, etc, at a particular instant/moment in time. Thus, cross sectional research is the equivalent of taking a photograph at a moment in space and time. As data or evidence collection can take weeks or even months there can be debate as to when a research project is truly cross sectional as opposed to longitudinal. However most empirical research is considered to be cross sectional. Longitudinal research studies consider an organisation, a person, a country, etc over a period of time but there is no specific agreement as to what time period needs to be involved before a study should be considered to be in the category.
154.	Cross-disciplinary	A study which draws on material which spans two or more fields of study.
155.	Cum laude	Latin term meaning *with praise*. Some universities make no distinction among the varying quality of research degree dissertations. The research

Glossary of Research Concepts and Issues

No.	Term	Definition
		degree is either awarded or it is not. Other universities will offer an outstanding graduate the honour of being awarded his or her degree with distinction. Other universities use the Latin terms cum laude, summa cum laude, maxima cum laude, magna cum laude to mark outstanding work.

Glossary of Research Concepts and Issues

D

Data to Duty of Care

No.	Term	Definition
156.	Data	Numbers, words, images, sounds or other sensory stimuli which cause a researcher to take notice and which he or she may or will use in his or her research process. It is important to note that the purpose of data is to help answer the research question and thus anything which does not contribute to this objective should not be considered as data but rather as noise.
		The word evidence is sometimes used interchangeably with data.
		Data is sometimes contrasted with information. Information can be described as data which has been processed or structured. Although this distinction may be useful in information systems for example, it is not of much value to academic researchers who are usually agnostic about perceived differences with regards to this issue.

Glossary of Research Concepts and Issues

No.	Term	Definition
157.	Data acquisition plan	Part of the research design which identifies the data required for the research and suggests where the data may be located and who might be able to facilitate access to this data.
158.	Data cache	Sources of data such as minutes of meetings, corporate press releases, corporate correspondence, newsletters, magazines and newspaper cuttings.
159.	Data curation	The management activities required to hold data and ensure its continued integrity.
160.	Data dredging	A term used to describe data mining without having first established a hypothesis which is to be tested.
161.	Data driven research	Sometimes researchers establish their research question as a result of having access to data. In such circumstances the researcher will examine the data in the hope of finding some patterns that will suggest a research question which should be of interest to the community.
162.	Data errors	There is always the possibility that data is incorrectly recorded or that mistakes occur when data is being processed. Such data errors can destroy the validity of the research.
163.	Data fracturing	This is a Grounded Theory Method term which points out activities such as data

No.	Term	Definition
		coding that tends to break data up and produces a range of data elements. In one sentence it is possible to find two or three or even four different variables or concepts being mentioned. These are individually coded and assessed before being brought together in a model or theoretical conjecture.
		Coding should be contrasted with a holistic approach to understanding data such as hermeneutics where whole sentences or even paragraphs may be understood as one concept.
164.	Data frequency table	This is an approach to summarizing data so that patterns within the data may be observed. Typically the number of times an observation occurs is counted and a table is created where observations are listed together with the number of their occurrences.
		For variables which have a large number of observations it is customary to group the outcomes into intervals and then to count the number of times an observation occurs within the interval.
165.	Data integrity	Academic research requires data to be relevant, accurate, unbiased and error free. It is also important that the data has been acquired using the highest research ethics principles. In general, no misrepresentations should be made to anyone supplying data for academic

Glossary of Research Concepts and Issues

No.	Term	Definition
		research. All of these issues are dimensions of the integrity of the data. Unless the researcher is confident of the integrity of the data it should not be used in academic research.
166.	Data management	Ensuring that the research data is correctly entered into an appropriate software package and that it is securely held with appropriate back up arrangements.
		Data management procedures include minimising the number of errors which can creep into data while it is being processed as well as ensuring that the provisions of the ethics protocol are complied with.
167.	Data mining	The interrogation of databases for the purposes of seeking relationships in the data. This technique is often associated with, or is an aspect of data driven research.
168.	Data orientated methods	Research methods which focus on the use of data to answer the research question. This is in contrast to theoretical research which uses ideas and concepts rather than primary data. http://bit.ly/1qeTDFT
169.	Data preparation	Data normally needs to be transferred from the initial medium on which it was captured to a medium suitable for analysis. In the case of questionnaires for

Glossary of Research Concepts and Issues

No.	Term	Definition
		example the answers to the questions normally have to be entered into a computer. In the case of interviews, the data may sometimes have to be transferred from a speech recording device to text before analysis can take place.
170.	Data protection	Academic researchers are required at all times to protect the data they have acquired. They need to ensure that it is held securely and that it is not accessed by anyone other than themselves and those working with them on their research project. Confidentiality is a key issue in academic research.
171.	Data Protection Act	The Law relating to how data may be acquired, recorded and used. It is essential that academic researchers familiarise themselves with this law and comply with the provisions of this act. Many if not most countries have data protection legislation and researchers should be familiar with its provisions.
172.	Data sampling	In most cases a researcher cannot collect all the relevant data which exists and which could help in answering the research question. There may be just too much data to handle within the parameters of the research project. Therefore the researcher will often, if not always, have to acquire a sub-set or sample of the data. The manner in which it

No.	Term	Definition
		is decided which sub-set to acquire is referred to as data sampling.
173.	Data saturation	In qualitative research a question which arises is how much data is necessary. This may be answered by using the concept of data saturation.

Data saturation occurs when the researcher ceases to obtain new insights into the possible answer to his or her research question when interviewing or obtaining evidence in any other way from informants.

Data saturation may occur after a relatively small number of data collection episodes, or it may require a significantly large number to be performed. This is usually a function of the complexity of the research question and the environment in which the researcher is working. |
| 174. | Data security | Issues relating to how data is stored in such a way that it is not available to anyone other than the researcher and his or her colleagues. Ethics committees are increasingly at pains to ensure that researchers keep personal data relating to informants in such a way that it will be safe from prying eyes. |
| 175. | Data set | A collection of data. |

No.	Term	Definition
176.	Data triangulation	Obtaining data from a variety of different sources in order to understand different perspectives on the research question. Data triangulation may use a variety of techniques to collect/produce evidence including interviews, internal reports, annual accounts, corporate press releases, stockbrokers' reports, the business press, etc. http://sociology.org.uk/
177.	Data types	Data may be categorised in a number of ways. The most fundamental categorisation divides data into quantitative and qualitative data. Within quantitative data there are 4 recognised data types which are nominal, ordinal, interval and ratio data. Within the qualitative data group there is text, verbal, visual, audio, tactile and olfactory data.
178.	Dataism	This refers to an attitude towards research which emphasizes the primacy of data in answering a research question. Except, perhaps for theoretical research, data is always central to research. However, the term dataism is reserved for situations where there is extra emphasis placed on all the processes associated with the acquisition, management and use of data such as in found in the Grounded Theory Method.

Glossary of Research Concepts and Issues

No.	Term	Definition
179.	Debriefing	On certain occasions ethics committees will give permission for a degree of deception to be used in a research project. When this occurs, the researcher will usually be asked to debrief the research participant immediately after the data has been acquired.
180.	Deception	Researchers are expected to be fully honest and open with research participants and everyone else associated with the research. Any form of deception is generally regarded as unacceptable. However, there are situations in which some deception might be tolerated such as research related to topics which delve into honesty. It would not be possible for example to study dishonest practices by asking individuals if they are dishonest. In general studies involving any deception are regarded with great suspicion by ethics committees.
181.	Deconstruction	The term is sometimes used to describe a philosophical movement started in the 1960s. However, it is also used in a broader sense to refer to closely examining a concept or a situation and considering its constituent parts in order to more fully understand its component

Glossary of Research Concepts and Issues

No.	Term	Definition
		elements and how they relate to one another.
182.	Dedication	Some researchers wish to dedicate their work to family members or others who have assisted them in their achievement. This is normally written on a separate page at the beginning of the dissertation.
183.	Deduction	A way of thinking and a way of approaching a research problem.
		The act of developing specific ideas or suggestions from an already established theory. Deduction is sometimes described as moving from theory to hypotheses. The hypotheses are then normally tested using data – often quantitative procedures are used, although not exclusively.
		Deduction is primarily a theory testing procedure although if the testing so dictates the results of a deduction exercise can lead to a modified theory or even a new theory. Any new theory so created will be inductive in nature.
		http://falcon.jmu.edu/~omearawm/deduction.html
184.	Defence (of the thesis)	The name given to the event in the USA whereby the work of a doctoral candidate is examined orally. The degree candidate defends his ideas and work in person to an examination panel. The

Glossary of Research Concepts and Issues

No.	Term	Definition
		term Viva Voce is also used to describe this event in some countries.
185.	Definition	An explanation of a concept in such a way that it is distinguishable from other concepts. A definition will often be expressed in relatively abstract terms. It is important to note that a definition is not an example which may sometimes accompany a definition.
		Some concepts (and even artefacts, events and entities) are difficult to define, and these are often better understood by offering a description. An excellent example of the problems which may be encountered with this is provided in the poem by John Godfrey Saxe, The Blind Men and the Elephant.
		http://www.constitution.org/col/blind_men.htm
186.	Delays	Academic research can encounter delays at a number of points. Sometimes supervisors can take months to review a final version of a dissertation. Although universities typically ask examiners to complete their report on the research within two months, examiners can similarly take many months to read a dissertation and offer a date for a viva voce.
187.	Deliberate interventions	Deliberate interventions are the basis on which experimental research is conducted. Deliberate interventions need

Glossary of Research Concepts and Issues

No.	Term	Definition
		to be contrasted with passive observation.
188.	Delimitations	Every research topic is required to have boundaries or limits which are described as aspects of the research question in which the researcher is interested, and which are contrasted with aspects of the research question in which the researcher is not interested.
189.	Delphi study	A systematic interactive approach to obtaining information from a group of knowledgeable informants. The knowledgeable informants are asked to score a set of statements regarding the future and the scores received from the whole group are calculated (with some analysis) and used as feedback to the group forming the basis of a second and third round of questioning. The purpose of a Delphi study is to establish to what extent there might be a degree of consensus among the knowledgeable informants. http://bit.ly/1lc9gib
190.	Democratising academic research	Before the acceptance of the Grounded Theory Method, it was accepted that the primary activity of novice researchers was the testing of already established theories. The development of new theories was not considered appropriate unless the researcher was already

Glossary of Research Concepts and Issues

No.	Term	Definition
		a well-established and respected academic researcher. The arrival and acceptance of the Grounded Theory Method allowed less experienced researchers to claim that they had developed a theory, albeit mostly a substantive theory. This has been described as the democratisation of academic research.
191.	Demographic	Descriptive aspects of an individual or a sample or a population which describe it such as age, gender, location, income, etc.
192.	Dependent variable	In the process of researching cause and effect situations some variables are considered to be independent and others are considered to be dependent. A dependent variable is one which reacts to changes in the independent variable.
193.	De-platforming	The withdrawal of an invitation to an invited speaker due to concern that his or her views may be politically incorrect. De-platforming or no-platforming as it is sometimes referred to has caused concerns about freedom of speech on campuses.
194.	Descriptive research	Academic research traditionally aimed to provide theories or explanations of the situations being studied. To achieve this there needs to be some starting

Glossary of Research Concepts and Issues

No.	Term	Definition
		point in the understanding of the topic being examined.
		Sometimes a researcher who is addressing a new topic will begin with a study which aims only to describe the context and/or outline the situation which will be researched in more detail later. This may be referred to as descriptive research.
195.	Descriptive statistics	Statistical techniques which allow the population for which data has been acquired to be described. These statistics will often be simple averages, but may also involve measures of dispersion. This approach to statistics does not lend itself to any inferences being made.
196.	Design	See *Research design.*
197.	Desk study or desk research	A research project which is conducted with reference to secondary data only. The secondary data will be accessed through already published material.
		http://www.resmind.swap.ac.uk/content/00_other/glossary.htm
198.	Detachment	A characteristic of academic researchers which suggests that they are not committed to confirming a particular point of view.
199.	Determinants of methodological choice	A researcher will normally choose his or her methodological approach based on one or more of the following factors:

Glossary of Research Concepts and Issues

No.	Term	Definition
		<ul><li>The nature of the research question,</li><li>The skills and former training of the researcher,</li><li>The attitude of the university at which the research is to be conducted,</li><li>The funding available for different types of research,</li><li>The encouragement of the supervisor.</li></ul>
200.	Determinism	Determinism is a philosophical stance which can be interpreted in a number of different ways. In the research domain determinism refers to a belief that if a research finding exists and is valid in one setting it will be so in another. Determinism also reflects the fact that it was believed that the world operated on clockwork principles which were the same throughout the whole universe. http://www.informationphilosopher.com/freedom/determinism.html
201.	Dialectic	The term dialectic may be traced as far back as Socrates and refers to a process of argument or debate. The dialectic consists of three steps. The first step is the postulating of a thesis. The thesis is considered by an intellectual opponent who points out its short comings and reformulates the thesis as an antithesis. The thesis and the antithesis are

Glossary of Research Concepts and Issues

No.	Term	Definition
		considered together, and this often leads to a synthesis which creates a new idea which may be postulated as a new thesis. This dialectic process may be repeated until the various parties feel that a consensus has been achieved.
		The concept of the dialectic was further developed by Hegel and by Marx.
		http://en.wikipedia.org/wiki/Thesis,_antithesis,_synthesis
		https://www.marxists.org/glossary/terms/d/i.htm
202.	Diary/ research journal	The keeping of a diary of research work is regarded as being important for competent research. The diary need not be completed every day but should record all important events and insights occurring to the researcher.
203.	Dilemma	A dilemma occurs when a researcher is faced with a difficult choice. For example a researcher might like to ask a personal question of an informant in order to clarify a situation but knows that it might offend him or her and this could lead to the informant withdrawing from the research altogether.
204.	Diminishing returns	The rule of data saturation is based on the law of diminishing returns which state that there is an optimal level at which an activity may be perused and that after that point the effort

Glossary of Research Concepts and Issues

No.	Term	Definition
		expended is not worth the return achieved.
205.	Discipline	The subject matter of a branch of knowledge. It implies that there are strict boundaries between branches of knowledge.
206.	Discombobulate	To confuse or to disconcert. If a researcher oversteps the mark and asks a question which the informant does not wish to answer he or she might obtain a reply which could discombobulate him or her.
207.	Discourse	Debate or discussion held to air differences in opinion. Discourse drives academic research through the process of the dialectic.
208.	Discourse analysis	A broad term which covers the study of interaction verbally, in writing or by sign language between individuals. Discourse analysis attempts to closely examine the meanings conveyed by exploring issues related to the words chosen, the structure of the sentences, the manner of the communication and other related issues. Social and cultural conditions play an important role in this type of analysis. Those interested in discourse analysis will be unsatisfied with any attempt to understand a communication on its face value alone. https://sites.google.com/a/sheffield.ac.uk/all-about-

Glossary of Research Concepts and Issues

No.	Term	Definition
		linguistics/branches/discourse-analysis/what-is-discourse-analysis
209.	Discrete variable	A discrete variable is one which cannot take any value within a range, but which is in some way limited to a number of possible values. Thus, a discrete valuable may be one which can assume any integer value (whole number) between 1 and 5 for example.
210.	Disinterested	The word disinterested is sometimes used to describe a researcher who has no biases and who is not trying to demonstrate a particular result through his/her research.
211.	Disinterested researchers	Academic researchers are sometimes described as preferably being disinterested in the findings of their research. This means that the researcher should not desire to have a particular outcome of the research, but rather be equally pleased at whatever the results of the research reveal.
212.	Dissemination	Research findings need to be made known to the community and the activity of making them known is referred to as disseminating the results. This is primarily achieved by publishing the results of research in academic journals and also though teaching and public lecturers and now the Internet.

Glossary of Research Concepts and Issues

No.	Term	Definition
213.	Dissertation	Written presentation of the research process, the research findings and its conclusion is usually required as part of a master's degree or a doctorate. Some undergraduate programmes now require short dissertations from their students. The word thesis is sometimes used as a synonym for dissertation especially at doctoral level. A dissertation may also be described as a monograph.
214.	Dissertation by papers	Doctoral research may be reported in two distinct ways. The first of these is by being written up in one book which is normally described as a dissertation or thesis. The other way of reporting research is through the writing of research papers which are intended to be published in academic journals. The regulations relating to the use of the research papers route to a doctorate vary considerably from university to university. It is sometimes suggested that the papers approach is in some sense easier than the dissertation or monograph route to the doctorate, but this is seldom the case.
215.	Dissertation publishing	If a particular research project is currently topical it may be possible to have the dissertation published as a monograph.

Glossary of Research Concepts and Issues

No.	Term	Definition
216.	Distance learning	A system of participating in an educational experience away from the university or institution at which the degree candidate is registered. Distance learning was initially conducted using traditional postal services but as telecommunications technology improved and e-Learning technology became more accessible, distance learning procedures have been applied. See *e-Learning*
217.	Double blind review	The reviewer does not know who the author is and the author does not know who the reviewer is. This type of review is required for papers proposed to academic journals which are peer reviewed.
218.	Dropout rate	In certain experiments or data collection activities a group or cohort of research participants or informants are required. When these research activities are conducted over a period of time it is often the case that certain individuals withdraw from the research activity. This is a common occurrence with a Delphi study for example. The proportion of the informants which withdraw is known as the dropout rate.
219.	Dualism	This term is used in several different contexts, but it often refers to Descartes' idea that the world should be

Glossary of Research Concepts and Issues

No.	Term	Definition
		understood in terms of its physical and intellectual dimensions. These were seen as two distinct domains. However it is increasingly accepted that these are highly interconnected in a number of different ways. Dualism is also used to describe the Yin and the Yang or the good and the bad etc. http://plato.stanford.edu/entries/dualism/
220.	Dumbing down	Expressing a concept in such a way that important aspects of the situation are removed from the explanation in order to produce a too simplistic view. See *Occam's razor*
221.	Duration of degree	Each university has regulations about the minimum duration for which a research degree candidate may be registered. The length for full time students is typically one year for a master's degree and three years for a doctorate. Traditionally there was no maximum period of registration but today most universities have a time limit on registrations.
222.	Duty of care	Part of the rationale of requiring researchers to seek permission to conduct research is that the university has a duty of care towards its researchers. Applications which suggest that the

No.	Term	Definition
		research will be conducted in dangerous environments will be either rejected or the researcher will be told to take various precautions before commencing the work.

Glossary of Research Concepts and Issues

EDAMBA to *Eyeballing the Data*

No.	Term	Definition
223.	EDAMBA	European Doctoral Programme Association in Management and Business Administration. A body created to support doctoral degree research.
224.	EIASM	European Institute for Advanced Studies in Management. A body created to support doctoral degree research.
225.	e-Interview	An interview which is not conducted on a face-to-face basis, but across the internet, perhaps on Skype.
226.	e-Journal	A scholarly publication carrying peer reviewed papers which is available on the web. e-Journals are sometimes available without charge to the reader.
227.	e-Learning	The application and use of Internet and web-based systems for the purposes of delivering and acquiring knowledge.

Glossary of Research Concepts and Issues

No.	Term	Definition
228.	Electronic submission	As well as submitting a dissertation on paper it is now increasingly common for universities to ask for an electronic copy to be delivered at the same time. The electronic copy is often tested using plagiarism detection software.
229.	Eligibility criteria	Researchers need to find knowledgeable informants who can supply data or evidence about the subject being researched.
		In order to ensure that appropriate data or evidence is acquired the researcher needs to be clear as to the type of informant who is in a position to supply this. The eligibility criteria will describe such a person.
230.	Emancipatory research	A term used in critical theory research. Emancipation from some unsatisfactory aspect of society is one of the key objectives of this research paradigm.
231.	Emergent research design	In contrast to the notion of a fixed research design an emergent research design is one which develops or emerges as the research proceeds. This is in fact a more realistic attitude toward the way in which academic research projects play out.
232.	Emic	Research conducted within the group focusing on how the group or the culture in which the research is being performed thinks about the topic. It is

Glossary of Research Concepts and Issues

No.	Term	Definition
		contrasted with an etic perspective which focuses on the researcher's perspective. See *Etic*
233.	Empirical generalisation	The term empirical generalisation is used in a similar way to the term hypothesis. The use of the word hypothesis is often reserved for quantitative research and the term proposition is used for qualitative research. If the theory to be tested has been developed as a result of empirical research, then the term empirical generalisation is used.
234.	Empirical research	The use of primary data as the basis of addressing the research question. Empirical research requires sense-based data, i.e. observation or accounts of those involved in the issues being researched, by which the research question may possibly be answered. http://plato.stanford.edu/entries/rationalism-empiricism/
235.	Empiricism	A philosophical stance which asserts that all knowledge is acquired directly by sense perception. It is only through our senses, and not through the received wisdom of others, that we can claim any form of knowledge. This being so then the

No.	Term	Definition
		researcher's first step is to acquire primarily data for him or herself.
		Empiricism was the main philosophical bedrock on which the modern scientific understanding of the world was based.
		However as simply stated empiricism has its limitations. It is not possible to directly perceive elections or even atoms. It is not possible to perceive gravity, or DNA, or justice.
		Nonetheless it is possible to research these topics by perceiving the direct effect of these phenomena.
236.	End game	During the final weeks of a research project there are a number of issues which have to be concluded and checked before the dissertation may be submitted for examination. This period of the research is sometimes referred to as the end game.
237.	End Notes	A software package available on a range of computers with which to manage a list of references. http://www.endnote.com/
238.	End noting	A form of referencing where the publishing details of the author being referred to are provided at the end of the paper or chapter or book. This is done by using a number which is inserted in the text of the paper or book and

No.	Term	Definition
		explained in the end notes which are listed in the order in which they are encountered in the text.
		This approach to reference is also referred to as the Chicago style.
		http://www.chicagomanualofstyle.org/tools_citationguide.html
239.	Enrolment	Some universities allow prospective students to enrol as a step towards formal registration. This status indicates that the students are active in the process of obtaining registration and gives them certain privileges such as access to the library.
		See *Registration*
240.	Epistemology	The study of the nature of knowledge and how it is acquired by individuals and society.
		Epistemology underpins many of the decisions which are made by researchers including the choice of methodology and the use of specific data collection approaches and data analysis techniques.
241.	e-Research	A set of tools available through the Internet such as Skype, Google (various products), Academic Earth, TED and many others which can facilitate researchers in their attempts to answer their research questions.

Glossary of Research Concepts and Issues

No.	Term	Definition
242.	Error term	In statistical modelling an attempt is made to express relationships between variables in terms of mathematical expressions. However mathematical expressions can obscure the variability inherent in the relationships between the variables. A way of accommodating this variability is to incorporate an error term. Thus, the model Y=mX+c may be more correctly expressed as Y=mX+c+e where the e represents the fact that there is variability or uncertainty in the equation.
243.	ESRC	Economic and Scientific Research Council which is a leading research and training agency which supports academic research in the UK. Most countries will have an equivalent of the ESRC and researchers are well advised to establish what assistance or support they can obtain from such bodies.
244.	Essentialism	A philosophical view based on Plato's Cave allegory or fable. According to this view every object and substance has, in its most basic form, essential characteristics. In normal life people do not see these characteristics, but rather a visible approximation. Plato tells us that we see life like people trapped in a cave who can only make out the shadow of objects and substances.

Glossary of Research Concepts and Issues

No.	Term	Definition
		http://www.lancs.ac.uk/staff/twine/ecofem/essentialism.html
245.	et al.	Latin term meaning *and others*. Used when referencing multiple authors.
246.	Ethical guidelines	The issues related to responsible conduct of research. These include matters which are not normally directly addressed by ethics committees. http://www.ncbi.nlm.nih.gov/pmc/articles/PMC3988765/
247.	Ethics	A branch of philosophy which is concerned with issues related to what is considered right and wrong. In academic research ethics normally refers to a code of practice which describes the type of research behaviour which is questionable or not acceptable to the research community.
248.	Ethics back dating	This occurs when a research project has been commenced without ethics approval. Most universities claim that they will not countenance ethics back dating but sometimes it is necessary when a project slips between the cracks in the ethics approval system.
249.	Ethics committee	A group of people holding a formal position within a university who review research proposals in order to attempt to minimize the university's exposure to

Glossary of Research Concepts and Issues

No.	Term	Definition
		any risk arising out of research conducted by its members or students.
		There are often a number of different ethics committees in a university with the highest level usually being a sub-committee of the University Senate which delegates responsibility to Faculties or Schools or Departments where there will be other ethics committees.
250.	Ethics protocol	An ethics protocol is a document which outlines how a research project will be conducted so that it complies with the rules and regulations imposed by the institution at which the research is being conducted.
		An ethics protocol will identify any potential ethical issues related to the research process, together with the way in which this potential ethical problem will be avoided or ameliorated. The ethics protocol is usually written by the research candidate and approved by an ethics committee. Data collection should not begin until the ethics protocol has been approved.
		http://www.edu.plymouth.ac.uk/RES-INED/beginning/begresed.htm
251.	Ethics refusal	This occurs when the ethics committee declines to give its consent to a research project.

Glossary of Research Concepts and Issues

No.	Term	Definition
252.	Ethics review board	This is sometimes the ethics committee sitting with a slightly different hat on whereby it is checking to ensure that the procedures agreed to when the ethics protocol was approved, were in fact followed.
253.	Ethics update	The ethics committee will give permission for a particular plan of research. However sometimes the research does not unfold in the way that was anticipated and the researcher may have to return to the ethics committee to update his or her plan and obtain permission to continue the research.
254.	Ethnography	A qualitative research approach which requires the researcher to become familiar with the lived experiences of the research subject/s. This technique is longitudinal in nature and thus requires the availability of a long period of evidence collection and understanding. http://bit.ly/1q1YFXg
255.	Ethnomethodology	An attempt to understand the workings of society from direct observation. It is a relatively new approach in the field of sociology.
256.	Etic	A scientific perspective used by anthropologists. It describes how the group looks to an outsider. Emic in contrast describes how the group looks to an insider.

Glossary of Research Concepts and Issues

No.	Term	Definition
257.	EUDOKMA	European Doctoral School on Knowledge and Management.
		An institution created to offer support to doctoral degree candidates across Europe.
		http://www.edamba.eu/r/default.asp?iId=GHMKJE
258.	Evaluation of research	Research findings are written up either in dissertations or in papers which are published in peer reviewed journals. Strict criteria are applied to such research before it is regarded as acceptable. The process of applying these criteria is sometimes referred to as the evaluation of the research.
		Research which has not been subjected to peer review or evaluation is generally not considered to be of much value.
259.	Evidence	The word evidence may be used as a synonym for data. Some academic researchers prefer the word evidence as it does not have the same connotation of authority as data and this is considered more appropriate for doctoral research.
260.	Evidence based research	Another way of describing empirical research.
		See *Empirical research*
261.	Ex cathedra	From the source of authority and thus difficult to question. This term originates from the period when all

Glossary of Research Concepts and Issues

No.	Term	Definition
		knowledge was derived from religious sources, especially from the Roman Catholic Church. The Pope and his hierarchy of cardinals disseminated accepted knowledge through the network of bishops and then on to priests who informed the laity. A cathedral was or is the seat of a bishop.
262.	Examination	In the context of research, masters and doctoral degrees are examined when the dissertation is finally submitted. In the case of the doctoral degree the examination is normally a two-part event in which the dissertation is assessed and the degree candidate is also evaluated during an oral interview which is referred to as a viva voce.
263.	Exemplary case study	A term used by Yin in this seminal text book on case study research. An exemplary case study is one which meets all or at least most of Yin's requirements. There are five general characteristics required for exemplary case study research and these are: the case study should be significant; it should be complete; it should consider alternative perspectives; it should display sufficient evidence; it should be composed/written in an engaging manner. http://www.ischool.utexas.edu/~ssoy/usesusers/l391d1b.htm

No.	Term	Definition
264.	Experiment	A demonstration or an investigation of the relationship among variables to look for support for an hypothesis or a theory. There are several different classes of variables and types of experiments. In most experiments the researcher is able to manipulate one or more of the variables.
265.	Experimental control	For an experiment to be accepted as a valid demonstration it has to be performed in compliance with a set of rules. These rules may be described as experimental control. www.mtsu.edu/~sschmidt/methods/**control**.html
266.	Exploratory research	An approach to research where there is not yet a large body of knowledge. Exploratory research is used to open up a field of study or a topic. Exploratory research is sometimes regarded as less formal and leading to results which may not be entirely consistent with sound research practice. http://www2.uiah.fi/projects/metodi/177.htm
267.	Extant literature	The body of academic literature is extensive both in terms of the large number of sources and also the fact that it has been accumulated over many years. Thus, on some topics there will be papers written 10 or 20 or even a 100

Glossary of Research Concepts and Issues

No.	Term	Definition
		years ago. Of course, there will also be papers and other documentary evidence which no longer exist. Literature which has survived and is still available may be referred to as the extant literature. The term is also used to describe the currently published and readily available literature.
268.	External examiner	Research degrees are normally examined by a number of academically qualified individuals. The number and the process of examination differ considerably from country to country.
		In many cases individuals who are not directly involved in the university awarding the degree are invited to be part of the examining group. Such examiners are referred to as external examiners.
269.	Eyeballing the data	The visual inspection of data which is normally performed before any formal analysis takes place. This eyeballing is normally used to seek evidence of trends in the data.

Glossary of Research Concepts and Issues

Facebook to Fuzzy logic

No.	Term	Definition
270.	Facebook	An early social media product which is frequently used by researchers to develop or participate in groups of interest to his or her research topic.
271.	Face validity	On the face of it, i.e. without thorough examination. Is the instrument valid and are prospective knowledgeable informants able to understand what is required by the questions?
272.	Face-to-face interview	A type of interviewing where the informant and the researcher meet in close proximity. Telephone and internet interviewing where the informant and the researcher do not meet are also sometimes used but of course are not regarded as face-to-face.
273.	Facile argument	An argument with little substance and which can be shown to be weak or irrelevant with comparative ease.

Glossary of Research Concepts and Issues

No.	Term	Definition
274.	Facilitator	A role required when conducting a focus group. The facilitator will ensure that the event runs smoothly. The main issues which a facilitator needs to be mindful of are that the discussion can easily drift off the required topic; an individual can dominate the discussion; unpleasant disagreements can occur; and the event can run over time.
275.	Factor analysis	A multivariate statistical technique which is used by researchers in order to identify how it is possible to understand different variables as part of more comprehensive factors or supra-variables.
276.	Facts	The term fact is normally used when the validity of a statement is being emphasized such as, "It is a fact that Charles Lindbergh was the first man to fly across the Atlantic Ocean single handed in 1927". However, facts may be challenged. Friedrich Nietzsche (1844 -1900) famously said, "There are no facts, only interpretations" A statement such as "It is a fact that Napoleon was the greatest Frenchman to ever live" could well be challenged. Academic researchers are well advised to avoid the word fact wherever possible. The 'fact' provided above about Charles Lindbergh may also be challenged.
277.	Fake journal	See *Hijacked journal*

Glossary of Research Concepts and Issues

No.	Term	Definition
278.	Fake News	Incorrect information or even deliberate lies propagated to deceive. As this appears to be on the increase it is essential that researchers do not take data at face value but insist on careful collaboration or verification of data.
279.	Falsification	A term proposed by Karl Popper which asserts that for a statement to be scientific it has to be expressed in such a way that it can be tested for validity and thus it is possible to falsify it.
280.	Fatal flaw	This term denotes the condition by which the research may be considered not to be of value. The flaw may be due to inappropriate conceptualisation of the research question, the acquisition of inappropriate data, the misuse of analytical techniques or the drawing of ill-considered conclusions.
281.	Feasibility study	An investigation in order to establish whether a proposed project could be usefully undertaken and whether suggested results are achievable.
282.	Feminist Research	Research which focuses on issues related to the role of women in society.
283.	Field experiment	A field experiment will attempt to simulate a laboratory experiment, but there will not be the degree of control which is achievable in a laboratory setting.

Glossary of Research Concepts and Issues

No.	Term	Definition
284.	Field Procedures	Set of activities required to collect data or evidence from informants. These range from making appointments, to understanding the dress code, to having a device to record interviews.
285.	Field notes	Personal notes made by researchers over and above the main collection of data from the informant. These are often quite informal.
286.	Field of study	The term field of study is sometimes used in place of what was previously called discipline. The word discipline is difficult as it implies specific boundaries which can be hard to define. A field of study may involve more than one traditional discipline. Many research projects involve complex fields of study which may include two, three or more areas of knowledge.
287.	Field studies	Research which is conducted outside of the library or the laboratory in a natural setting. There is a wide range of environments in which field studies may be conducted which includes collecting data by questionnaires, holding focus groups, being involved in participant observer work to mention only a few.
288.	Field test	Before using a questionnaire or an interview schedule (i.e. a research instrument) it is useful to test it on a small

Glossary of Research Concepts and Issues

No.	Term	Definition
		number of respondents. This is also referred to as a pilot test.
		Such tests are quite formal and should be conducted with participants who will be similar to those with whom the research instrument will eventually be used.
289.	Findings	The results of the analysis of the data collected and/or the synthesis of the ideas used in a theoretical research project. The objective of an academic research project is to produce a finding or findings.
290.	First draft	A research dissertation will often go through several drafts before it is finalised. A first draft will be incomplete, but it will give the researcher a boost to know that he or she is well on the way to completing the work.
291.	Fit	A grounded theory method term referring to whether a theory corresponds well to a situation which it purports to explain.
292.	Fixed design	Traditionally researchers were expected to specify a research design at the time they prepared their research proposal. It was then thought that the research design was fixed and that the course of the research would follow the suggested design.

No.	Term	Definition
		This notion of a fixed design seldom reflected the actual course of the research project.
293.	Flexible design	A research design which points to the general direction of the research, but which is intended to allow the researcher to easily respond to discoveries during the research process.
294.	Focus group	A group of individuals assembled so the researcher can observe a discussion on the research question. The individuals need to be knowledgeable about the subject of the research and a facilitator needs to keep the discussion on track. Focus groups should consist of between 4 and 6 participants and should last between 45 minutes and 90 minutes.
295.	Fog index	A measure of how difficult it is to read and understand a paper or a book or any other form of text. The Gunning fog test is a frequently used index of readability. http://www.readabilityformulas.com/gunning-fog-readability-formula.php
296.	Follow up research	A research design can have multiple phases which may be based around some sort of before and after intervention. The second and subsequent phases of such research can be referred to as follow up research.

Glossary of Research Concepts and Issues

No.	Term	Definition
297.	Foot noting	A form of referencing where the publishing details of the author being referred to are provided as a footnote to the page on which the authority has been referenced. This is done by using a number which is inserted in the text of the paper or book and explained in the foot note. See *End-noting*
298.	Formal theory	A theory which is applicable to a number of different situations and/or organisations and/or individuals. Thus, formal theory has a wider scope than substantive theory.
299.	Formative evaluation	A process of evaluating a situation or a person and in so doing offering advice as to how to improve the situation. Formative evaluation is orientated towards how to make improvements rather than simple assessment.
300.	Frankfurt School	A group of interdisciplinary social theorists originally based at the Institute for Social Research at the Goethe University in Frankfurt dating back to 1923. The ideas of the Frankfurt School have been adopted by some individuals throughout the research world. Researchers following this train of thought may also be referred to as critical theorists. These researchers are concerned with social change. They explore the establishment of new and more rational

No.	Term	Definition
		institutions. They emphasize the critical component of theory development to overcome the limitations of the more conventional approaches to social research. http://en.wikipedia.org/wiki/Frankfurt_School-cite_note-Held.2C_David_1980.2C_p._15-5
		Critical theory is a specialised and controversial branch of academic research.
		See *Critical theory*
301.	Fraud	A deliberate misrepresentation which is intended to mislead either a research or those who are participating in the research. When findings are published which are the result of falsified data or wilfully biased procedures they may also be regarded as fraudulent. Fraud is not the same as mistakes.
		Such an activity could have legal implications.
302.	Fudging references	The practice of claiming to have read an author when only a reference to that author in another publication has actually been seen. The fudging of references is considered to be an unethical practice.
303.	Full time	The traditional designation of university studies was either full time or part time. Full time generally meant that the degree candidate did not have any other

Glossary of Research Concepts and Issues

No.	Term	Definition
		form of employment and was expected to spend the full day engaged with his or her studies.
		Today there are additional designations such as distance learner or e-learner.
304.	Fuzzy logic	Whereas traditional logic relies on categorical statements which are regarded as true such as *all cats have whiskers,* fuzzy logic employs statements which are not categorical or always true in the same way as the above example. In fuzzy logic one speaks about intermediate truths as well as absolute truths. Thus, in fuzzy logic it is recognised that some propositions may be truer than others or that their truth content needs to be qualified in some way. Fuzzy logic is a relatively new topic which has been successfully applied in some situations, but which is in need of further development. http://www.seattlerobotics.org/encoder/mar98/fuz/flindex.html

Glossary of Research Concepts and Issues

Gatekeeper to Guess

No.	Term	Definition
305.	Gatekeeper	An individual or an organisation which exerts some control over the researcher's access to knowledgeable informants.
306.	Generalisability	The ability to claim that a research finding is applicable to other locations and instances than the one at which the research was conducted. Research findings are sometimes thought to be either generalisable or not generalisable whereas in reality research findings may be in some respects/degrees generalisable and in other respects not.
307.	German neo-Kantianism	A research orientation which emphasises idiographic study which is detailed study of small samples rather than nomothetic study of mass data. The idea springs from Kant who said "ultimate reality" is inaccessible to us ... a sufficiency of understanding rather than a totality of understanding is what we can aim for and sometimes achieve.

Glossary of Research Concepts and Issues

No.	Term	Definition
308.	Ghost writing	The employing of others to write academic work for the purpose of having it fraudulently presented under another name.
309.	G-Index	A measure of the productivity and impact of a scholar's work. A G-Index of n is acquired when n papers have been cited n times in other scholarly journals. See *H-Index*
310.	Glossary	A list of word, terms and phrases with their accompanying explanations.
311.	Goodwill	A positive attitude to academic reviewing. It is difficult to imagine an academic research output which is perfect or even near perfect. There are nearly always a number of things that can be done to improve the results of the research. Within the academic community it is expected that any research report be approached with an attitude which first looks for the positive side of the work. Goodwill is related to respect.
312.	Grab	A Grounded Theory Method term referring to the extent to which a newly developed theory will have resonance with the researcher's community.
313.	Gradualism	The idea that material progress towards a set of objectives can be achieved by slow but consistent movements in the right direction.

Glossary of Research Concepts and Issues

No.	Term	Definition
		Academic research is sometimes said to be based on a gradualist philosophy in that it takes time to reflect on and understand the issues and concepts involved. It can also be necessary to be involved for an extended period before the "penny drops" and the issues become clear to the researcher.
314.	Graduation	The ceremony at which the degree is conferred upon the students who have complied with all the necessary regulations of the university. A graduation ceremony is sometimes referred to as the Commencement. See *Commencement*
315.	Grand Theory	A term which is used to contrast the level of theory developed by those using the Grounded Theory Method and the theories developed by the famous theorists such as Adam Smith, Karl Marx, Henri Fayol, Max Weber and John Maynard Keynes to mention only a few.
316.	Granularity	The level of detail to which a system is reduced in order to conduct a research project. Thus, studying organisations holistically would be one level. Studying their marketing policies would be another and studying their product development procedures would be another.
317.	Grey documents	A term used to refer to textual material which has not been produced by a

No.	Term	Definition
		formal publishing organisation, such as notes, consultants reports, correspondence or minutes of meetings etc.
318.	Grounded Theory Method	Grounded Theory Method is an inductive, theory discovery methodology that allows the researcher to develop a theoretical account of the general features of a topic/situation while simultaneously grounding the account in empirical observations or data. (Glaser, B. and Strauss, A. (1967) The Discovery of Grounded Theory: Strategies for Qualitative Research. Aldine, New York.)
		Grounded theory is an important element of much of social science theory although it is not often specifically articulated as such.
319.	Grounds for failing a research dissertation	A research dissertation may be failed if the examiners are of the view that it has not made an adequate contribution to the field of study and/or it is inadequately scholarly.
		A dissertation will also be failed if any misconduct such as plagiarism is detected.
		See *Cheating*
320.	Group dynamics	Individuals can behave quite differently in a group compared to how they would behave as individuals. Furthermore, certain individuals can inordinately influence a group. It is important to be

No.	Term	Definition
		aware of these aspects of group dynamics when conducting a data collection activity such as a focus group.
321.	Group effect	Data or evidence may be collected from a group as is common practice using a focus group. When this technique is employed it is important to be aware that opinions may be formed as a reaction to what is being said in the group rather than the considered view of individuals.
322.	Group interview	The interviewing of several informants simultaneously. Group interviewing is sometimes confused with focus groups which is a different process of data collection.
323.	Guess	Research using a deductive approach normally starts with a theory from which the researcher develops hypotheses which are then tested. Sometimes these hypotheses are informally referred to as guesses.

Glossary of Research Concepts and Issues

Halo effect to Hypothetico-deductive research

No.	Term	Definition
324.	Halo effect	A false impression which may be obtained from certain individual informants who appear to be more informed than perhaps they really are.
325.	Hard data	Numeric data is sometimes described as hard data, and this is contrasted with non-numeric data which is sometimes referred to as soft data. Hard data is often based on assumptions which can be quite soft in practice.
326.	Harvard referencing system	A set of rules used to ensure that a reader will be able to find a source document to which reference has been made in a piece of academic text. It is also known as the author date system or the parenthetical referencing system. It uses the surname and the date of publication of the authority in the text and full details, listed in

Glossary of Research Concepts and Issues

No.	Term	Definition
		alphabetic order by lead author are provided at the end of the document. This system of reference is thought to have been initiated at the end of the 19th century, but it was only referred to as the Harvard system in the late 1940s.
327.	Hawthorn Effect	This term was coined in the 1950s, but it refers to an experiment which was conducted in the 1920s at the Hawthorn Plant of the Western Electric Company near Chicago.
		In this experiment workers were encouraged to increase their productivity and one of the ways in which this was done was to improve the illumination in their working environment. As the lighting was improved so their output improved.
		However, at some point it was decided to reduce the illumination and this had the surprising effect of the productivity continuing to improve.
		This led to the belief that the improvement in productivity was due to the management's concern for the workers and their environment rather than the amount of light supplied and is generally referred to as the Hawthorn Effect.
		http://en.wikipedia.org/wiki/Hawthorne_effect

Glossary of Research Concepts and Issues

No.	Term	Definition
328.	Heisenberg effect	The very fact that research is taking place can change the practices within an organisation.
329.	Hermeneutics	The study of the theory of interpretation. It includes both verbal and non-verbal communications. Hermeneutics draws on a number of different frameworks including alethic, objectivist, critical, double, etc. http://plato.stanford.edu/entries/hermeneutics/
330.	Heterogeneity	This term refers to the degree of uniformity. A substance or a group is Heterogeneous if there is a high degree of difference among the elements thereof.
331.	Heuristic	A rule of thumb. A shorthand approach to solving a problem or making an estimate based on experience.
332.	Hijacked journal	A website which purports to be part of an established academic journal, but which is actually a fraudulent representation and is in fact a predatory journal.
333.	H-Index	A measure of the productivity and impact of a scholar's work. It is based on a set of the scholar's most cited papers. The H-Index reflects the number of citations the scholar's work has received in other publications. See *G-Index*

No.	Term	Definition
334.	Historicism	Historicism suggests that all human activity is defined by its history and that the human condition can only be understood in terms of its history. Human activity builds on and reacts to what has been before. The notion of the social contract is central to this thinking. Historicists therefore see empiricism as being misguided due to its lack of concern for contextual- historical issues and its emphasis on reductionism. They assert that the Zeitgeist is a critical issue which needs to be incorporated in any understanding of the situation. https://www.princeton.edu/~achaney/tmve/wiki100k/docs/Historicism.html See *Zeitgeist*
335.	Historiography	The methodology employed by historians in the study and research of their field. This term is also used to refer to the history of the study of history. http://qcpages.qc.cuny.edu/writing/history/critical/historiography.html
336.	Holism/Holistic	An approach to research which is based on understanding an individual or an organisation as a whole. A holistic view would claim that studying the parts of a phenomenon would not lead to an adequate understanding of the whole.

Glossary of Research Concepts and Issues

No.	Term	Definition
		Holism is seen as the opposite of reductionism.
337.	Holistic evaluation	An evaluation of an event, a situation, an individual or group as a whole. Such an evaluation would focus on a single measure or a group of measures but would make a broad assessment.
338.	Homogeneity	The degree of similarity in a substance or a group. Something is homogeneous if there is a high degree of similarity among the elements thereof.
339.	Honest cheater	A term that is an oxymoron. However, it is sometimes used to describe self-plagiarism which occurs when a researcher publishes the same material more than once purporting it to be different work.
340.	Honorary doctorate	A doctorate awarded by universities in recognition of the achievements of an individual. Such a doctorate could be offered for any reason including community service, outstanding research, and political influence to mention only a few. Honorary doctorates are not normally awarded for academic prowess.
341.	Honours	This has a number of different meanings in the academic world. An honours degree is one which has required the degree candidate to specialise in a subject to a level beyond that which is required by a general degree. Honours may also

Glossary of Research Concepts and Issues

No.	Term	Definition
		refer to the awarding of a degree cum laude etc. See *Cum Laude*
342.	Human centred	Research that is focusing on the needs of people rather than systems or processes.
343.	Hybrid research	A combination of different research methodologies and methods to answer a research question. This is also referred to as mixed methods research. Although this is increasingly popular there are a number of practical and theoretical problems with this approach to research. http://www.socialresearchmethods.net/tutorial/Sydenstricker/bolsa.html
344.	Hyper-complex	A term used by the famous Harvard Professor of biology Edward Osbourne Wilson to describe social science.
345.	Hypothesis	A claim made by a researcher which requires testing to see if it can be falsified or rejected. An hypothesis needs to be stated in such a way that it is possible to be rejected.
346.	Hypothesis testing	The way in which researchers attempt to refute an hypothesis. An hypothesis test will involve a null hypothesis and an alternative hypothesis. If the null

Glossary of Research Concepts and Issues

No.	Term	Definition
		hypothesis is rejected then the alternative hypothesis is accepted pro tem. http://www.stats.gla.ac.uk/steps/glossary/hypothesis_testing.html#hypothtest
347.	Hypothetico-deductive research	Term sometimes used as a synonym for positivist or quantitative research, and is based on deduction and the testing of hypotheses obtained there from. http://www.philosophyprofessor.com/philosophies/hypothetico-deductive-method.php

Glossary of Research Concepts and Issues

I

Ibid to ISSN

No.	Term	Definition
348.	Ibid	Latin term meaning *in the same place*. This is used in the process of referencing an authority in a paper or dissertation. Ibid means that the reference where this word is used is exactly the same as the one immediately above.
349.	Idealism	A philosophical stance which asserts that the world is really composed of ideas rather than objects. It may be contrasted to the view of materialists who believe that the material or physical manifestation of objects is the only issue of importance.
350.	Idiographic study	Small sample research or unique event research is sometimes referred to as being idiographic. Thus, the use of a small number of case studies could be referred to as an idiographic study. http://www.answers.com/topic/idiographic

No.	Term	Definition
351.	Imagination	It has been commented on primarily by Richard Feynman that the processes of research are relatively straight forward and that the greatest challenge to the researcher is to have the imagination to identify really interesting research questions.
352.	Impact factor	A measure of how often a journal is referenced by authors in their published works. The impact factor is the average number of times in a given year that citations of the papers in the journal were made during the two preceding years. It is regarded as a measure of how important the journal is to the academic community. http://www.sciencegateway.org/impact/
353.	Imputed response	Questionnaires are sometimes returned with some questions not answered. When this happens, some researchers will attempt to guess what the response of that informant might have been. When this occurs, it is said that the researcher has imputed a response to the question.
354.	In viva codes	Codes used in the process or characterising of data and the concepts therein which are based on actual words used by informants.

Glossary of Research Concepts and Issues

No.	Term	Definition
355.	Inclusion criteria	The conditions under which an informant should be included in a sample. This may also apply to a case study.
356.	Independent variable	Some research projects examine the relationship between an input factor and an output situation. An example of this could be the amount spent on different forms of advertising and the resultant effect this has on sales income. In such a situation the input factor is the amount spent on advertising and is referred to as the independent variable; the sales income is understood to be the result of this expenditure and is called the dependent variable.
357.	Indexing	The creating of a means of rapid access to information, either by establishing a list, as is customary at the end of a book or by creating a database with computer codes or keys.
358.	Indexing service	An organisation which indexes academic publications and provides rapid information about them. This service is normally supplied at a cost. The organisations which index academic journals attempt to ensure that a minimum standard of academic quality is maintained by the journals indexed.
359.	Induction	One of the two principal approaches to academic research. Induction proceeds

Glossary of Research Concepts and Issues

No.	Term	Definition
		by moving from data to theory, i.e. the researcher formulates a theoretical conjecture as a result of reflecting on the data collected. Induction is normally but not exclusively part of a qualitative research process.
		Induction needs to be contrasted with deduction. See *Deduction*.
		http://www.bfi.org.uk/education/teaching/researchguide/pdf/bfi-edu-resources_research-the-essential-guide.pdf
360.	Inference	A claim which is based on either data or evidence or as a result of logical deduction.
		Inference is closely tied to theory development which is the objective of academic research.
361.	Inferential statistics	When statisticians use data from a sample — a subset of the population — to make statements about a population, they are performing statistical inference. This involves estimating values accompanied by a statement concerning the uncertainty associated with it.
362.	Informant triangulation	By obtaining data from multiple informants the researcher may be able to obtain a richer picture and thus understanding of the situation being studied.

Glossary of Research Concepts and Issues

No.	Term	Definition
		Different informants will have different points of view.
363.	Information	In practice the term information is often used interchangeably with data and evidence. However, it has been argued that information is the result of the processing of data. Information helps to reduce uncertainty about a situation, an object or a process.
364.	Information fatigue	By being exposed to a large amount of information it is possible that a researcher becomes overwhelmed and errors occur. It is of course difficult to know when enough information has been acquired to make a sound informed judgement.
365.	Instagram	A social media application for the purpose of sharing photos and video.
366.	Instrument error	Perfect measure is impossible. Even in the purely physical world if three engineers measure a length they will inevitably produce different results, even if the differences are minute. In social science there is concern that a measuring instrument such as a questionnaire could have built in flaws which prevent it from performing the task which it is supposed to be undertaking. If this happens then it is said that there is an instrument error.

No.	Term	Definition
367.	Instrumentalism	This concept is used in different ways by different researchers. It usually denotes a belief in a focused approach to achieving an objective and takes a pragmatic outlook on the processes involved. The term instrumentalist is used to describe a researcher who has made instrumentalism a key aspect of his/her research.
		http://www.answers.com/topic/instrumentalism
368.	Integrity of research	This refers to a constancy of values, methods, actions and principles which are applied to the research. It also refers to the care and attention given by the researcher to ensure that no accidental errors are allowed to creep into the research. If the integrity of the work is not maintained then the findings are regarded as suspect.
369.	Intellectual capital	The wealth of knowledge and experience which a researcher will bring with him or herself to the research question.
370.	Intellectual property rights (IPRs)	Legal entitlements concerning the ownership of the results of intellectual achievements or creations of the mind.
		IRPs may have artistic, scientific and commercial implications.
		There can be tensions between the university and its graduates as to who has priority with regard to IPRs.

Glossary of Research Concepts and Issues

No.	Term	Definition
371.	Intellectualisation of method	The term used to describe how it is now necessary, especially in the social sciences, to justify research methods in terms of our philosophy and values.
372.	Inter alia	Latin term meaning *among other things*.
373.	Inter-subjectivity	The notion of objectivity is difficult to define and even more difficult to operationalise. When a statement such as, *Objectively women do not run as fast as men*, is made, what it really means is, *Let us agree, women do not run as fast as men*. Some researchers argue that this type of statement is not well described using the word objectivity but that the term inter-subjectivity is a better description. The term inter subjectivity recognises that there are many different ways of perceiving the world around us and that frequently objectivity only refers to consensus among experts.
374.	Interdisciplinary	Drawing from two or more original disciplines. This term is sometimes used as a synonym for multi-disciplinary.
375.	Internal consistency or Reliability	Used to assess the consistency (in the sense of stability) of results across items within a test. It is a concept which is often used in statistical analysis by calculating correlations between different variables. Cronbach's alpha is one of the measures used for this.

Glossary of Research Concepts and Issues

No.	Term	Definition
		http://en.wikipedia.org/wiki/Internal_consistency
376.	Internal examiner	Degree examiners from within the university or institution awarding the degree.
		In some institutions the candidate's supervisor may become an internal examiner.
377.	Internal validity	Required in cause and effect research ….. Is the cause being studied really that which is responsible for producing the effect observed?
		http://www.socialresearchmethods.net/kb/intval.php
378.	Internet interviewing	The term internet interviewing could be applied to both email exchanges and also the use of audio or video conferencing systems such as Skype. A series of questions put and answers obtained across an internet connection. This should be contrasted to face to face interviewing.
379.	Inter-Observer Reliability	Used to assess the degree to which different raters/observers give consistent estimates of the same phenomenon.
380.	Interpretivism	Interpretivism is a school of thought which looks beyond numerical representations of phenomena and tries to explain and therefore understand issues

Glossary of Research Concepts and Issues

No.	Term	Definition
		underpinning or driving complex situations.
		In research it is generally accepted that "facts" do not speak for themselves. The more often used word data (instead of fact) is also understood as needing processing and explanation before it can be usefully seen as a contribution to the answering of a research question.
		Interpretivism is the approach to research whereby the emphasis is placed on the need to take care with the meaning of words, actions and situations by providing a full explanation of what is actually happening and what are the intentions of the key actors.
		http://www.encyclo.co.uk/define/Interpretivism
381.	Interval data	Interval data provides a continuous scale on which to mark or assess an occurrence. On this scale the difference between two adjacent numbers is regarded to be the same. Thus, the difference between 2 and 3 is regarded to be the same as between 3 and 4.
382.	Interview	A meeting between a researcher and a knowledgeable informant whereby the researcher seeks to obtain data related to the research question. It is said that there are two philosophical approaches to interviewing. The first is when the

No.	Term	Definition
		researcher is using a mining framework, i.e. the researcher believes that the informant has "the answer" which is being sought. The second is where the researcher sees himself/herself as a traveller and it is not assumed that he/she will have an answer.
383.	Interview schedule	A list of questions which will be used during an interview with an informant.
384.	Interview script	A set of guidelines which an interviewer will have with him or her to guide them through the process of conducting the interview. It may consist of questions, prompts and other notes
385.	Introspection	See *Reflection*
386.	Investigator triangulation	By obtaining data through the use of multiple investigators or researchers a study may be able to obtain a richer picture and thus understanding of the situation being investigated. Multiple investigators will bring different points of view with regard to how the research question may be answered.
387.	Irreducible ambiguity	It is one of the primary objectives of academic research to illuminate ambiguity wherever possible. This is especially true in the publishing of results. However, no matter how hard the researcher tries there are situations where this may not be possible. In such

Glossary of Research Concepts and Issues

No.	Term	Definition
		situations it may be argued that the ambiguity is irreducible.
388.	ISBN	International Standard Book Number based on a 13-digit code which uniquely identifies a published text. Having an ISBN is a prerequisite for a piece of work to be recognised by the academic community.
389.	ISSN	International Standard Serial Number (used for journals).

Glossary of Research Concepts and Issues

Jargon to Journal

No.	Term	Definition
390.	Jargon	Specialised vocabulary used by individuals who have been initiated to the subject area.
391.	Journal	A published periodical which reports the research of scholars in a certain field of study. To be valued by the academic community journals need to be peer reviewed, i.e., assessed by other scholars of equal standing.

Glossary of Research Concepts and Issues

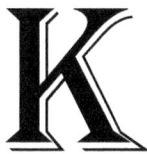

Key informant to Knowledgeable informant

No.	Term	Definition
392.	Key informant	An academic research project will inevitably require data or evidence from multiple informants. Not all informants are equal as some will be more knowledgeable than others and some will be more prepared to share their knowledge than others. Those informants who are especially knowledgeable and who have been helpful are sometimes referred to key informants.
393.	Key words and phrases	A collection of words or phrases used to allow computer searches to locate a paper or a dissertation in a database.
394.	Knowledge	In a broad sense knowledge may be regarded as an awareness of, or a familiarity with, or an ability to understand a topic. Knowledge may be acquired through either formal means such as education or through experience.

No.	Term	Definition
		A distinction is often made between information and knowledge. A hierarchy ranging from data to information to knowledge to wisdom in the form of a pyramid has been suggested.
		In the academic world knowledge often has a more theoretical orientation. The objective of doctoral research is often expressed as adding something to the body of knowledge. In this context knowledge actually refers to a theoretical or abstract explanation of a phenomenon being studied.
		See *Theory*
395.	Knowledge café	A gathering of individuals with a common interest who are prepared to explore ideas surrounding a topic through conversation to obtain a more complete understanding of the issues involved.
396.	Knowledge claim	The output of academic research is the addition of something of value to the body of theoretical knowledge. This output may be regarded as a knowledge claim.
397.	Knowledge creation	The object of academic research. It means that something new is discovered and in the context of academe it required an addition to be made to some aspect of theory in the field being researched.

Glossary of Research Concepts and Issues

No.	Term	Definition
398.	Knowledgeable informant	An individual who has the data/evidence/knowledge which the researcher seeks. Only knowledgeable informants should be approached to supply data/evidence/knowledge to the research.

Glossary of Research Concepts and Issues

Leading question to Longitudinal research

No.	Term	Definition
399.	Leading question	A leading question is one where the researcher is prompting the informant to provide the sought after answer. An example of such a question is, "Do you not really feel that a murderer should get life in prison?"
400.	Learning research	The final purpose of all research is to learn and in so doing add something of value to the body of theoretical and practical knowledge. However, although it is a central issue the learning of the researcher him or herself is sometimes overlooked. The research process itself teaches the researcher as he or she moves from step to step sometimes in a cycle of improvement. This occurs especially in qualitative research where the researcher increases his or her understanding as the data or evidence is collected.

Glossary of Research Concepts and Issues

No.	Term	Definition
401.	Learning logs	A record of what the researcher has been learning during the processes of the research experience.
		This is a useful source of data when reflecting on the research findings.
402.	Length of dissertation	Doctoral dissertations are frequently, in the British university system, around 80,000 words. However professional doctorates can be shorter.
		Master's degree dissertations are normally under half this length.
		Masters by course work dissertations are even shorter. Sometimes only 10,000 words are required for these dissertations.
403.	Letter of consent	A written statement from informants to the effect that they are voluntarily participating in the research. This letter will also point out the rights of the informants and the conditions under which the data will be held.
404.	Library research	Research conducted on secondary data which is accessed through resources supplied by a library.
405.	Likert scale	An ordinal psychometric scale developed by Rensis Likert in 1932. It is often presented as a 5-point scale ranging from strongly agree to strongly disagree. It is an ordinal scale where only the 5 points are available. Likert scales

No.	Term	Definition
		or a derivative there from are used extensively in the social sciences.
		However, the data collected from these scales has often been treated as though it was generated from a continuous interval or ration scale.
406.	Limitations	Every research project and the resulting findings will have limitations due to time pressures and cost constraints. Limitations should be explicitly stated in the report of the research.
		There may be other limitations due to such factors as access to informants as well as to other types of data which could have improved the researcher's understanding of the situation
407.	Limits to knowledge	Sometimes the question is asked, "Is there a limit to human knowledge?" Clearly there is no answer to such a question. There are several reasons why this is a problematic question and perhaps one of the most difficult is that it is not possible to know what we do not know and therefore we will not be able to know if we have ever reached the limit of knowledge in any normal understanding of the words.
408.	Literature	The body of published work, normally referred to as papers in peer reviewed journals. Sometimes research books and articles published in non-reviewed

No.	Term	Definition
		journals or newspapers may be regarded as part of the literature. Academic literature is normally an account of research conducted by the author/s which has answered a research question.
409.	Literature review	A critical description of the contemporary and relevant body of relevant published material describing the current state of knowledge of the topic being researched. It is an essential part of any programme of academic research and frames the context of the research. The literature review is also used to validate the methodology.
410.	Logic	The use of valid reasoning to move one's thinking from opening assumptions or assertions to useful conclusions. It is to do with the way an argument is crafted. The use of logic is often equated to being rational. However, it is difficult to define a rational argument.
		Logic has been studied from ancient times across the world civilizations and despite this it remains a difficult topic.
		The rules of logic have been described as the laws of thought.
411.	Logical positivism	A term which originates from the Vienna Circle which was formed in the early years of the 20th century. It is a school of philosophy which combines

Glossary of Research Concepts and Issues

No.	Term	Definition
		empiricism with aspects of rationalism. It is a form of what it normally referred to simply as positivism. The term is seldom used today.
412.	Logical chain of reason	In an academic research project, each step or phase should lead onto the next in a way that is obvious to the researcher's community. There should be no leaps of faith in the research design. All arguments produced should be based on authority, data or agreed logic.
413.	Longitudinal research	Research which is conducted over an extended period of time. There is no simple answer to the question of how long a study should be before it is considered to be longitudinal.

Glossary of Research Concepts and Issues

Mail questionnaires to Multivariate analysis

No.	Term	Definition
414.	Mail questionnaires	Questionnaires are produced on paper and distributed and normally retrieved by the postal system. This approach is not used much anymore.
415.	Making contact	Obtaining access to appropriate informants is an important issue in academic research and making contact with these individuals is a skill which needs to be cultivated by researchers. Sometimes the best strategy for making contact is to find a gatekeeper who can introduce the researcher to the informants required. See *Gatekeeper*
416.	Management	The research degree candidate's ability to manage his or her time as well as the resources which the university puts at his or her disposal.

No.	Term	Definition
417.	Management guidelines or management policy	The outcome of an academic research degree was traditionally the requirement that it should add something of value to the body of theoretical knowledge.
		However, in recent years with the articulation of the distinction between mode 1 and mode 2 research, social science faculties are increasingly looking towards research degrees to also offer some insights which have practical management value. This is sometimes referred to as management guidelines or management policy suggestions.
418.	Mass observation	A movement in the UK which tried to observe the everyday life of the citizens of the country without informing the citizens that they were objects of research. It began in 1937 and continued until the 1950s.
		The project was resuscitated again in the 1980s. It is based at the University of Sussex who hold the archive of the material collected by this process.
419.	Materialism (Physicalism)	A philosophical view which believes that the most important driver in the state of the world and the affairs of humans is the physical or material nature of the objects which are found in the environment. It is things that are most important and they determine much of our attitudes and values. At some levels

Glossary of Research Concepts and Issues

No.	Term	Definition
		this view is clearly important and relevant as the technology available to society highly influences social thinking and processes. But there are other important non-physical drivers which materialism tends to ignore. Materialism may be contrasted with idealism.
420.	Mathematical induction	The traditional technique used by mathematicians whereby a proposition is proved to be true for a number of values, normally for the values of 1, n, and n+1. If this is the case then within the assumptions of mathematics the proposition is regarded as having been proved. Mathematical induction is quite different to induction as a research design.
421.	Mathew effect	In the sociology of science it is known that success leads to more success. In practical terms this means that successful researchers are offered more grants, attract more students, and find more interesting problems than others. This phenomenon was described in the Judeo-Christian holy books by St Mathew who said that "Unto him that hath shall be given, from him that hath not shall be taken". Marx modernized this view by writing "The rich grow richer and the poor grow poorer".

No.	Term	Definition
422.	Maturity of researchers	Academic research is challenging in a number of different ways. It requires a high level of intellectual involvement, considerable energy and interpersonal skills. The degree of interpersonal skills in turn requires a high level of maturity especially with regard to acquiring qualitative data. This involves dealing with interviewing informants, conducting focus groups and other personal contacts.
423.	Mean	The average value in a data set. A simple mean is the total value of the data points divided by the number of data points. There are more sophisticated variations of this simple mean which involve weighting the data points in some way. Mean, average and central tendency are often used as synonyms.
424.	Meaning	There is always the question to what extent it is possible for a researcher to understand the intention of the creator of a communication. Thus, the question has to be asked *what was the meaning of the data which was supplied by the informant during the interview?* Or what *was the real intention of the press release?* It is possible that a communication could have a different meaning to the observer than was originally intended. Thus, ascertaining meaning can be challenging.

Glossary of Research Concepts and Issues

No.	Term	Definition
425.	Measure of dispersion	The degree of variation in a data set which is normally calculated by the standard deviation.
426.	Measurement	The systematic use or assignment of numbers to represent attributes of a situation, a phenomenon or a characteristic of a variable or construct.
427.	Measuring instrument	A device for the collection of data in order to test an hypothesis or a theory. Strictly speaking a watch, a ruler and a micrometer screw gauge are measuring instruments. In social science a questionnaire is a commonly used measuring instrument.
428.	Median	In a data set the median is the data element for which there are an equal number of data points with a higher value and lower value. It is the middle point in the data set.
429.	Mental model	A conceptual framework or explanation about how something works which exists in the mind of the researcher. By its nature a mental model is an abstract precursor of a more tangible representation of the issues under consideration. A mental model may be further developed for example into a physical model such as a miniature building or into a mathematical model in a computer.
430.	Mentor	An individual who offers general support and guidance to a student with

Glossary of Research Concepts and Issues

No.	Term	Definition
		their studies or research. Some universities use mentors in addition to supervisors for master's and doctoral degrees. Occasionally mentors are also used to assist members of staff integrate into academic life.
431.	Meta-analysis	An analysis of analysis. This usually involves the bringing together of several studies and performing an overreaching analysis of them as a whole.
432.	Metadata	Metadata is data about other data. Metadata can be used to summarise data but it is also useful in describing how data has been structured and or collected and stored.
433.	Metaphor	A figure of speech which compares something to another concept or object. For example, "*My determination to pass the examination was as if my life depended on it*", is a statement employing a metaphor.
434.	Metaphysics	A philosophic study of issues which are said to exist beyond or above physical being. Metaphysics transcends traditional fields of study. Metaphysics addresses fundamentally difficult to answer questions and as such it tends to have a special status in philosophy.
435.	Meta-theory	A theory of theories.
436.	Method	A term normally used to describe in detail the various ways in which data may

Glossary of Research Concepts and Issues

No.	Term	Definition
		be collected and processed and interpreted by the researcher. There are a large number of methods available to the researcher including questionnaires, interviews, focus groups, ethnography, longitudinal studies etc.
437.	Method of inference	When data has been collected it will need to be processed and inferences will normally be drawn. The data does not speak for itself. If the data is numeric then statistical techniques may be used to develop inferences. If the data is qualitative then a different set of inference procedures are required. Thus, the method of inference needs to be matched to the data type.
438.	Methodological choice	Every researcher has to choose how he or she will conduct their research. There are a large number of options available from which to select the most appropriate approach. These include taking a theoretical approach or an empirical one. Within empirical research there are two major choices which are positivism and interpretivism. Within these two categories there are numerous sub-categories.
439.	Methodological pluralism	Using more than one methodology in a single research project. This is a way of obtaining access to multiple lenses through which to acquire different perspectives regarding the research

No.	Term	Definition
		question and its possible answers. As methodologies tend to have rather porous boundaries many research projects can be envisaged as employing some degree of methodological pluralism. However, there are some researchers who suggest that a research project should be conducted by the application of one research paradigm. Such an argument would regard a combination of methodologies to be a mistake as it would reflect a confusion at the ontological level. For those who take this point of view mixed methods research is a methodological heresy.
		On the other hand many researchers are content to conduct their research using a methodological pluralism approach to their research in which multiple methods are acceptable.
440.	Methodological triangulation	The use of different underpinning theories with which to study a research question.
441.	Methodology	A high-level description of the framework within which the research will be conducted. It directly reflects the researcher's ontological and epistemological stances. There are a relatively small number of methodologies available to a researcher including a theoretical approach, an empirical approach, positivism, interpretivism, a critical theory

No.	Term	Definition
		framework, critical realism approach and mixed methods. Methodology should not be confused with method which refers to the details of the way the research will be conducted with particular emphasis on data collection, analysis and interpretation.
442.	Mind mapping	A graphical technique used to explore ideas or to arrange ideas in an easily understandable way. It may be used to facilitate a literature review or the writing up process.
443.	Miner metaphor	This term is used in relationship to the use of interviews for the purpose of collecting data or evidence. When a researcher believes that an informant knows the answer to a question which will lead to his or her being able to answer the research question, the researcher is said to be employing a miner attitude or using a miner metaphor.
444.	Mini-dissertation	Increasingly research activities are being included in the curriculum of undergraduate degrees and honours degrees. The output at this level of research is sometimes referred to as a research report or a mini-dissertation. The objective of this level of research is to understand a material amount of the relevant literature and to show some ability to critique it.

Glossary of Research Concepts and Issues

No.	Term	Definition
445.	Misconduct in science	A range of activities which are regarded as improper by the research community. These include undue bias, plagiarism, falsification of data and references, undue outsourcing, misrepresentation of the work done, including informants whose knowledge is suspect.
446.	Missing data	It is unlikely that all the possible relevant data can be collected for a research project. Researchers need to be cognizant of the fact that there will almost always be some missing data.
447.	Missing data	The data acquired for a research project is often incomplete. For one or other reason there will be potential data which has not been accessed. This may be considered as missing data. When it comes to issues related to incomplete questionnaires researchers sometimes try to impute values for missing data.
448.	Mixed Methods	A term which has a similar meaning to hybrid research i.e. this research will use more than one research methodology and more than one research method. http://mmr.sagepub.com/cgi/content/short/1/2/112
449.	Mode	In statistics the mode is the most frequently occurring data point.

Glossary of Research Concepts and Issues

No.	Term	Definition
450.	Mode 1	A term which has been used to describe the traditional approach to academic research. In Mode 1 research the research question needs to be found in the academic literature. It is not acceptable for the research question to arise in a practical environment. A Mode researcher will typically have only one supervisor. The researcher will not be encouraged to create his or her own network of contacts and they will typically not have tested their theses with anyone other than the supervisor before the examination of the work.
451.	Mode 2	A term which has been used to describe a more modern approach to academic research where strong emphasis is placed on the relevance of the research. This approach to research does not involve any compromise with regard to rigour but the research needs to clearly demonstrate that the findings are of value in use.
452.	Model	A representation of reality in such a way that we can understand its components and how it functions. Models may be physical such as an architect's model of a building; they may be on paper such as a blue print for a machine; or they may be mathematical and possibly be expressed through the operation of computer software.

Glossary of Research Concepts and Issues

No.	Term	Definition
453.	Moderator	In the academic context a moderator is usually an individual who reviews a situation and comments on its appropriateness. Examination scripts are often reviewed by a moderator to ensure that the expected standard is being applied.
454.	Modernism	In the context of research, modernism refers to an understanding of research methodology and methods which occurred after the principles and processes of research established by Galileo, Newton and others were understood and accepted. Modernism means an acceptance of the scientific method with an emphasis on objectivity (minimising bias), logic, reductionism and determinism.
		Modernism has driven science and technology since the 18th century and many would argue that it is directly responsible for the materialist progress made in the 20th century.
		Modernists believe that their approach to science will lead to an increasing improvement in understanding and control of our environment, in turn leading to a better life for all.
		The term modernism is also used in the pictorial arts world to describe some of the paintings produced by artists in the late 19th and early 20th century.

Glossary of Research Concepts and Issues

No.	Term	Definition
		See *Premodern* and *Postmodernism*
		http://witcombe.sbc.edu/modernism/roots.html
		http://www.youtube.com/watch?v=BT7ZIfPkVXI&NR=1
455.	Modus operandi	Latin term meaning *method of work* which can also be referred to as MO.
456.	Monograph	A dissertation is sometimes referred to as a monograph in that it is one large piece of work written by one author. The term is also used to describe a general book which has been written by one author and addresses one topic. When a dissertation is subsequently published in the form of a book it is often referred to as a monograph.
457.	MOOC – Massive Open Online Course	An open access educational event including video lectures and other course work which is available to anyone who wishes to participate.
458.	Motherhood	A platitude or a statement with which everyone would agree. Platitudes should not be included in any academic research findings. An example of a motherhood is the statement, "Competent managers perform better than incompetent ones".
459.	Multi-disciplinary	An integrated mixture of disciplines whereby each of the disciplines

No.	Term	Definition
		involved retains its own original methodological independence.
		See *Trans-disciplinary*
460.	Multi-methods research	There is some controversy about the use of this term. Some researchers use it as a synonym for mixed methods while others regard it as a separate concept. Those who make the distinction claim that mixed methods is the approach being employed when both quantitative and qualitative data is used in the same research project and multi-methods occur when different forms of the same type of data i.e. either qualitative or quantitative are engaged for the one project.
		If interview data and focus group data was used in a research project, then this could be referred to as a multi-method piece of research.
461.	Multiple interviews	This term is ambiguous. It can refer to a collection of separate interviews, but it can also be used to describe interviewing more than one person at a time. Interviewing more than one person at the same time is not generally regarded as sound academic research practice.
		See *Group interviews*

Glossary of Research Concepts and Issues

No.	Term	Definition
462.	Multiple triangulation	Using a number of different approaches to triangulation to provide a richer picture of the situation being studied.
463.	Multiple case study research	At doctoral level it is common to find research projects in which more than one case study has been employed. However, as case study research is intensive there will normally only be a small number of cases involved.
464.	Multiple researchers	Traditionally academic research for the purposes of a degree is expected to be conducted by one person only. Joint research is unusual. However, under certain circumstances some universities will allow a joint dissertation to be submitted.
465.	Multivariate analysis	Statistical methods for examining more than one independent variable and/or more than one dependent variable or both.

Glossary of Research Concepts and Issues

N

Narrative to NVIVO

No.	Term	Definition
466.	Narrative	A story or an account normally given either verbally or in writing by one person about a situation, a place, a concept or an individual.
467.	Narrative enquiry	A form of qualitative research in which narratives or stories about the subject of the research are collected and analysed in a holistic way.
468.	Natural experiment	A natural experiment takes place when a non-deliberate intervention occurs within a system which the researcher may use to understand the subject of his/her research. An often-cited natural experiment occurred when Mt St Helens exploded. This provided extensive information for environmental and ecological scientists who had recorded conditions on the mountain before the explosion/eruption and who were interested in how the environment would respond to the disruptive effect on flora and fauna living in the vicinity

Glossary of Research Concepts and Issues

No.	Term	Definition
		In social science the case of the separation and the subsequent clashes between the two groups known as the Maori and the Moriori and described by Jarred Diamond in Guns Germs and Steel (1997), published by WW Norton is often cited as a natural experiment. http://history-nz.org/moriori.html
469.	Naturalism	Suggests that social science should be studied in the same way as the "natural" sciences i.e. the physical sciences. http://plato.stanford.edu/entries/naturalism/
470.	Naturalistic enquiry	A general term which is used to describe an approach to research which does not follow a positivistic design, especially one based on laboratory experiment, but rather explores issues in their natural environment or setting. Naturalistic enquiry will tend to be interpretivist by nature.
471.	Negative examples	In order to be confident of a research finding, researchers sometimes look specifically for disconfirming evidence which could indicate the need to revise the findings. Disconfirming evidence may be referred to as negative examples.
472.	Negotiating access	Sometimes researchers are able to negotiate access to organisations by

No.	Term	Definition
		agreeing to allow the management of the organisation to have early access to the findings of the research. However, the academic researcher should not be perceived as an agent of management who is collecting information for the organisation. See *Access*
473.	Neo-pragmatism	Pragmatism which began in the 19th century became unfashionable in the middle of the 20th century. Neo-pragmatism is a revival of some of the original ideas of pragmatism which picked up some renewed momentum towards the end of the second half of the 20th century. Neo-pragmatism has stronger post-modern tendencies than the original pragmatism authors. The leading proponent of this was Richard Rorty.
474.	Network	In the context of research, the word 'network' refers to a group of people or institutions which have a shared interest in the research being conducted.
475.	Neutral stance	This term suggests that the research has not given support to or been influenced by a particular philosophy or set of values.

Glossary of Research Concepts and Issues

No.	Term	Definition
		This stance also suggests that the researcher will not have any personal agenda in conducting the research.
		It is generally believed that most researchers cannot be entirely neutral.
476.	Nice-to-know information	Information which a researcher might regard as interesting, but which does not directly or indirectly answer the research question.
477.	Noise	Sometimes relevant data can be confused with other facts and figures which do not contribute anything to the answering of the research question. Noise is sometimes defined as irrelevant or confusing data.
478.	Nominal data	Data that refers to descriptions rather than numbers. In a questionnaire the indication that the respondent was English speaking, for example, would be an element of nominal data.
479.	Nomothetic study	Large sample research is something referred to as being nomothetic. Nomothetic research needs to be contrasted with ideographic research which uses small samples. It has been suggested that nomothetic research will have a more general application than ideographic research.
480.	Non-academic audience	The findings of the research should be of interest to the widest possible community. This may consist of individuals

No.	Term	Definition
		who do not have any direct contact with universities. It may be useful for the researcher to communicate the results of the research to the media.
481.	Non-disclosure agreements	The supply of data to researchers by informants has both personal and commercial implications. With regard to personal implications the researcher is required to state explicitly that individual confidentiality will be respected. In addition, some organisations will require researchers to provide an assurance of non-disclosure of corporate information which could be regarded as commercially sensitive. The researcher may be asked to sign a formal agreement in this respect.
482.	Non-parametric statistics	Non-parametric statistics is an approach to the use of statistical analysis which is not based on parameterized families of probability functions and distributions. This approach to statistics may be used with data which is not interval or ratio in nature.
483.	Non-statistical arguments	Non-statistical arguments are made through the application of logic or reason. Such arguments do not employ numbers. Non-statistical arguments may be formal and thus use the structured rules of logic such as syllogisms or they may be less formal.

Glossary of Research Concepts and Issues

No.	Term	Definition
484.	Normal distribution	The normal distribution is a continuous probability distribution which describes the theoretical probability of different observations occurring if a distribution is normal. The normal distribution is generally represented as a bell curve whose actual shape is determined by the mean and the standard deviation.
485.	NU*IST	A software package designed to assist in the storage, management and understanding of qualitative data. Once the data has been entered and coded the computer allows quick and easy interrogation including cross tabulation.
486.	Null Hypothesis	In hypothesis testing a researcher establishes an hypothesis which is a claim which could be correct given that the theory on which it is based is correct. The researcher then attempts to reject this claim or hypothesis. It is important to note that there is never an attempt to prove an hypothesis. The hypothesis being tested is referred to as the Null Hypothesis and if it is rejected then the researcher agrees to accept pro tem the alternative hypothesis.
487.	Nuremburg code	An early attempt to establish a set of research ethics principles.
488.	NVIVO	A more advanced and easier to use version of NU*IST

Obfuscate to Oxymoron

No.	Term	Definition
489.	Obfuscate	The deliberate attempt to be less than open and frank with a researcher.
490.	Objective of research	Also referred to as the goal of the research. In simple terms the primary objective of a research project may be described as the answering of the research question. However more generally academic research is about describing and understanding the world, i.e., adding something to the body of knowledge in order to improve how we exist.
491.	Objectivity	The state of mind which an academic researcher is encouraged to have whereby he or she does not have a favoured outcome for a research project. Being objective means trying to minimise any biases the research may have.
492.	Observation	Seeing, hearing or sensing data relevant to the research. An observation is the identification of an occurrence of the subject being researched. In general, this term has a large semantic footprint

Glossary of Research Concepts and Issues

No.	Term	Definition
		and may be used in many different circumstances. An observation needs to be distinguished from noise which is the collection of data which is not useful in the answering of the research question.
493.	Occam's razor (Also spelt sometimes Ockham)	The belief that a simple explanation is often more satisfactory and useful than one which attempts to take into account all the possible variables and factors. This principle is used to support the notion of parsimony and is sometimes referred to as the Law of Parsimony. Einstein picked up on this idea and stated that "make things as simple as possible, but not simpler". Einstein was cautioning against *dumbing down*.
494.	Off books	This term is sometimes used to describe an abeyance situation whereby the research is suspended or paused for a period. See *Abeyance*
495.	One-to-one interviewing	This is normally understood as face-to-face although telephone interviewing and internet interviewing are becoming more prevalent.
496.	Ontology	The study of the nature of being. The two most basic positions in ontology are that we understand the world as either a real, materialistic and objective place totally governed by the laws of nature. This is described as realism.

Glossary of Research Concepts and Issues

No.	Term	Definition
		Alternatively, we recognize that every individual can only know the world through his or her own experiences or own perspective. The latter is called relativism or perspectivism. A leading proponent of perspectivism was Friedrich Nietzsche who famously argued that there was no such a thing as fact but only interpretations. There are many subcategories in realism and relativism. http://en.wikipedia.org/wiki/Ontology
497.	Op cit	In the work already cited. An abbreviation for the Latin *opere citato* meaning in the work quoted.
498.	Open access publishing	The traditional model for academic publishing was that the results of research, after the work had been double blind reviewed, were published in paper journals which were bought by universities and by individuals at a considerable cost. In general authors did not pay to have their work published, although some small journals did require authors to make a payment as their subscription fees were inadequate to cover their costs. These were known as page charges. As the Internet and the web became available some papers were uploaded on the web and made available to readers free of charge.

Glossary of Research Concepts and Issues

No.	Term	Definition
		There are now a growing number of journals, primarily available on the web, which can be accessed without charge. In these cases the authors are asked to pay a fee to cover the cost of the electronic publishing processes and these fees can vary substantially. Some academics have shown concern that the reviewing process for these journals may not be as thorough as it is for traditional journals. This new approach is referred to as open access publishing.
499.	Open coding	The attribution of codes (numeric or alpha-numeric) in order to fracture or parse data in order to be able to summarise the findings of the research. Open coding is the term used to describe codes which are allocated during the first pass through the data.
500.	Open ended question	An unstructured question which allows an informant the opportunity to provide a detailed answer.
501.	Open source	Universal access to software with a licence to use without any associated cost. It is based on the notion of collaboration between developer and users of software products.
502.	Opportunistic research	The identification and the execution of any aspect of a research project which the researcher pursues due to some serendipitous thought or encounter.

Glossary of Research Concepts and Issues

No.	Term	Definition
503.	Opportunity sampling	Like a convenience sample this represents data being collected when it is easy to do so. This type of data does not have a high status in academic research and is regarded as anecdotal at best.
504.	Ordinal data	Data which is presented in an ordered fashion usually indicating preference or importance. The numbers assigned to the outcomes indicate the order of importance. One of the characteristics of ordinal data is that it is not usually possible to be certain of the meaning of the differences between different points on the scale. For example, using an ordinal scale of 1 to 9 a questionnaire might require an informant to indicate how strongly he or she supports a management intervention. The question then becomes: Is the difference in preferences between a score of 3 and 4 the same as the difference in preference between 7 and 8? There is also the issue that some informants would not ever score a preference of 9 out of principle whilst others would have no problem in so doing.
505.	Originality	A piece of research is said to be original if its findings lead to a new or novel way of looking at the situation being studied. Research may also be said to be original in the way in which it has been

Glossary of Research Concepts and Issues

No.	Term	Definition
		conducted. Original research is not a repetition or replication of some previously performed work.
506.	Other academic outputs	Besides the production of a dissertation or thesis document, the work concluded as part of an academic degree can be reported through the delivery of seminars, conference presentations and papers some of which could be published in journals.
507.	Outlier	An observation which is distinctly different to all the other observations experienced during the research.
508.	Outlier	An outlier is an observation or data point that is numerically distant from the rest of the data set of which it forms part.
509.	Outlier processing	Decisions have to be made with regard to outliers. If an outlier is a genuine value which reflects the nature of the population then it should be incorporated in any statistics or description of that population.
510.	Outsourcing	Certain routine aspects of academic research may be contracted out to others to perform. This is referred to as outsourcing. The key issue here is that none of the intellectual content of the research should be outsourced.

Glossary of Research Concepts and Issues

No.	Term	Definition
511.	Ownership of the research	There are several different ways in which this term is used. The researcher needs to see the research project as being his/hers in order to have the commitment and the energy to complete the project. In another sense the ownership of the project can refer to the individual or institution holding the Intellectual Property Rights (IPRs).
512.	Oxymoron	A figure of speech which appears to be contradictory. Examples of oxymora include, clearly misunderstood, deceptively honest, deafening silence.

Glossary of Research Concepts and Issues

Page layout and font sizes to Puzzle solving

No.	Term	Definition
513.	Page layout and font sizes	Although each university will have its own specific rules regarding page layout and font sizes issues, in general dissertations are required to be printed in black ink on white paper, one and a half spaced, single-sided using a recognised type font, often 12 point.
514.	Panel study	A research project which utilises the views of individuals who have been selected as a panel to represent a particular sub-set of society.
515.	Paper concept note	A structured approach to thinking about the activities required in planning and developing a peer reviewed paper. It is a high-level design incorporating many of the activities required to achieve this objective.
516.	Paradigm	This word is sometimes used interchangeably with theory or model. It was popularised among scientists by

Glossary of Research Concepts and Issues

No.	Term	Definition
		Thomas Kuhn, who used it in his book *The Structure of Scientific Revolutions*. Kuhn's use of the word most closely resembles theory.
517.	Paradigm shift	A term coined by Thomas Kuhn to describe a new mind set brought about by the collapse or the abandonment of an established but outdated theory.
518.	Paradox	A paradox occurs when the conclusion of a series of rational concepts/ideas/statements leads to a contradiction. Despite the contradiction the result of the argument/s may still be correct.
		It is normally a situation which defies intuition and it may be irreconcilable.
519.	Paradox – Parmenides versus Heraclitus	At the very heart of research there is a paradox which has been identified by the ancient Greek and clearly expressed in the teachings of Parmenides versus Heraclitus.
		Parmenides argued that there was nothing new under the sun. This idea was supported by the ancient Hebrew scribes who made the same comment in Ecclesiastes. Modern thermodynamics also supports this notion in the First Law of Thermodynamics.
		Heraclitus on the other hand pointed out that all things are in flux and that nothing should be regarded as constant.

Glossary of Research Concepts and Issues

No.	Term	Definition
		Heraclitus illustrated this idea by commenting on the fact that one cannot fall into the same river twice.
		The paradox is that while at one level everything always remains the same at another level nothing is ever quite the same as it was before.
520.	Parallel-forms reliability	A concept used to assess the consistency of the results of two tests constructed in the same way from the same content domain.
521.	Parsimony	This term is usually used with reference to academic writing and it expresses the need for concise expression on the part of the author. There is no academic credit given for any form of long-windedness. It is a direct consequence of Occam's razor.
		See *Occam's razor*
522.	Part time	The designation applied to a student who is not full time. This implies that the student is employed in some other activities besides his or her studies. There are no guidelines as to how many hours per period would be regarded as part time as opposed to full time study.
		See *Full time*
523.	Participant information sheet	A document which is supplied to potential informants before they are asked to sign a letter of consent. The participant

No.	Term	Definition
		information sheet describes what the research is about; why the potential informant has been identified as a suitable informant; what he/she can expect to be asked to do and how the data they supply will be treated.
524.	Participant observer research	A researcher who involves him/herself in the organization or group which he/she is researching. A participant observer plays a dual role whereby he/she engages in some activity with the organization while at the same time observes what is happening for the purposes of his/her research.
		The participant observer keeps a detailed journal or diary and this becomes an important source of the material to be analysed together with other documentation.
525.	Participatory action research	For a research project to be considered a participatory action research event it would need to comply with the concept of action research as well as involve a team who participate in the research project on an equal or shared basis.
		Action research tends to involve individuals on this type of basis.
526.	Passive observation	Research based on observation without influencing what is being observed. An ornithologist in a hide is attempting to be a passive observer.

Glossary of Research Concepts and Issues

No.	Term	Definition
		When it comes to social science some researchers claim that passive observation is not actually possible. In any event ethics committees would no longer permit anyone to be a research participant without providing informed consent.
527.	Pattern	Academic research often looks to discover connections among variables. The connections are described as being patterns.
528.	Paying for information	It is increasingly difficult to find research participants who are prepared to offer their time to academic researchers. As a result, a payment is sometimes offered to those who are prepared to be involved with an experiment or who will complete a questionnaire. The proposed payment is sometimes offered in terms of a raffle for a prize. In general, this type of incentive is not thought to be good academic practice.
529.	Pedagogy	The study and theory of teaching.
530.	Peer review	The term peer review is an important construct in academic practice which is not always well understood. Academic output has to be evaluated and the process whereby research output is evaluated is generally referred to as peer review. Papers which are sent to academic journals for possible publication

No.	Term	Definition
		are said to be peer reviewed. But the word peer implies that the reviewer has the same academic status as the author. This is not always the case. In fact, it is difficult to imagine how equal status researchers could be found and successfully matched.
		It is sometimes said that the examination of doctoral research is in a sense a peer review in that the degree is awarded if the degree candidate can demonstrate that he or she is a peer of the examiners.
		See *Blind reviewing*
531.	Personal skills	An academic researcher needs to be adept at a range of activities which may include interviewing, data analysis, perceptual mapping, writing, to mention only a few.
532.	Phenomenology	This term is used in a number of different ways. Firstly, phenomenology is a philosophical stance developed in the early part of the 20th century in Germany concerned with the study of consciousness and the way that phenomena are perceived by the conscious mind.
		Secondly phenomenology is also a term which is sometimes used as a synonym for interpretivist research. In this sense it is the study of experiences collected

No.	Term	Definition
		in the form of spoken, observed or written evidence, i.e., qualitative data which is interpreted by the researcher. Using the term in this way may be confusing as the terms qualitative and interpretivist research are more generally understood. http://plato.stanford.edu/search/searcher.py?query=Phenomenology http://www.iep.utm.edu/phenom/
533.	Philosophical assumptions	Every research instrument and every approach to the collecting and analysis of data has at its roots a set of philosophical assumptions and/or values. A common philosophical assumption is that it is possible to understand the world around us. A value to which most academic researchers would prescribe is that it would be advantageous for us to be able to add to the body of knowledge. It is important to be aware of our assumptions and values in order to understand the implications of the research approach and findings.
534.	Philosophical high road	It is sometimes argued that there are "better ways" of doing research. When this is said it is usually suggested that the scientific method is the

No.	Term	Definition
		philosophical high road to sound research. This is not accepted by all researchers.
		The term *philosophical high road* suggests that there is some privileged way of understanding the phenomena being studied. In fact research methodology and research methods compete with each other for credibility. The methodology and method which deliver the most convincing argument are considered to be the best explanation/understanding we have pro tem.
535.	Philosophy	Philosophy refers to the study of central or foundational beliefs and issues. Philosophy carefully and critically examines definitions of concepts and analyses and the implications of the understandings acquired there from. It is a subject for which a significant level of maturity is usually required.
		All research activities are underpinned by a philosophical stance concerning the nature of knowledge and how it is possible to claim that research has led to the development of new knowledge. http://www.iep.utm.edu/
536.	Pilot study	A small-scale test to ensure that the researcher's ideas are likely to produce a viable data set with which to answer the research question.

Glossary of Research Concepts and Issues

No.	Term	Definition
537.	Piltdown Man	Scientific fraud claiming that the missing link between apes and humans was identified by some small remnants of skull bones discovered at Piltdown in Great Britain. It has been suggested that the fraud was perpetrated as a prank by Sir Arthur Conan Doyle.
538.	Plagiarism	The use of the ideas or words of others without adequate attribution. Plagiarism is considered by academics to be a violation of the trust which academics have in each other. Increasingly universities are requiring students to submit an electronic copy of their work so that it may be tested for Plagiarism.
		An act of Plagiarism would normally result in a disciplinary enquiry into this cheating conduct and this could lead to the degree candidate's registration being revoked.
		In recent years extreme forms of plagiarism have been uncovered where individuals have submitted complete dissertations to which they have claimed authorship, but which have been the work of others.
		See *Self plagiarism*
539.	Plagiarism testing	There are several software products available which will check a piece of text or a whole dissertation for any signs of

Glossary of Research Concepts and Issues

No.	Term	Definition
		plagiarism. Universities are now extensively using these types of checkers.
540.	Podcast	A digital audio file which may be streamed or downloaded for subsequent use.
541.	Political correctness	Academic research is subject to political correctness in the same way as all other aspects of our lives have become. However, in addition sometimes research has been questioned because of the gender or ethnicity of authors in the review and also for not reflecting appropriate diversity in the choice of informants.
542.	Posit	A synonym for assertion or claim, an example of which would be, "I posit that all men are equally susceptible to flattery".
543.	Positioning of perspective	In qualitative research there are many different ways of approaching the research process. In fact, the term qualitative research is problematic for a number of reasons including the fact that it may be used as a generic descriptor for such a wide range of quite different research attitudes, mind sets and methods. When qualitative research is reported in either a dissertation or in a peer reviewed journal the researcher's position as regards his/her approach needs to be explicitly stated.

Glossary of Research Concepts and Issues

No.	Term	Definition
544.	Positivism	A form of empiricism which believes that all knowledge is acquired by the application of the scientific method. Positivist research is sometimes referred to as hypothetical-deductive research as it is normally based on establishing hypotheses and testing them. Positivistic research will mostly be quantitative in nature and will be seeking to establish cause and effect relationships. The notions of reductionism and determinism are key positivist tactics. Positivists will argue that in performing their research they are able to dispel any personal biases they have.
545.	Post Hoc	Latin term meaning *after this*. For example "We were able to say post hoc that the interview with the managing director was most worthwhile".
546.	Postmodernism	As a starting point postmodernism is a philosophical orientation towards knowledge, society and research which has developed as a result of reflection on and critique of modernism. Postmodernism rejects the belief in a grand narrative for society leading to a better state of existence through an increasing understanding of the world. Postmodernism questions most of the assumptions which underpin normal research such as objectivity, the appropriateness of reductionism, and the meaningfulness of determinism. Postmodernists

No.	Term	Definition
		are critical of the application of the scientific method to the study of people and organisations in the social sciences. http://www.youtube.com/watch?v=oL8MhYq9owo&feature=related http://www.colorado.edu/English/courses/ENGL2012Klages/pomo.html
547.	Post-positivism	A term sometimes used as a synonym for interpretivism. Post-positivists argue that the scientific method is not often appropriate for the study of people and organisations.
548.	Pragmatism	An orientation towards knowledge and the creation thereof which arose in the United States of America during the second half of the 19th century. It has been seen as having more practical value than the highbrow debate on the nature of knowledge which was prevalent in Europe at that time. Pragmatism is a philosophical position taken by researchers that was named by Charles Sanders Peirce in which it is said, "What works is in some sense right". Also, what is useful is "true" or perhaps more appropriately for the 21st century, "What is useful is right". This philosophy was further developed by William James and John Dewey. According to the pragmatists the practice of

No.	Term	Definition
		enquiry is a social activity. There is always a problem behind research and the objective of the research is to solve the problem. Research is in a sense a transaction – an ongoing state of inquiry with changing evidence and changes in what we could consider as evidence. Warranted assertions, competent inquiry and knowledge are outputs of the research. An important test of validity in business and management research is whether or not the findings are regarded by the community as being useful.
549.	Praxis	There are several possible meanings associated with this Greek word. In academic research the term is normally used to describe the practical application of theory.
550.	Predatory journal	A fraudulent journal which purports to operate with the standards of an academic journal, but whose objective is to fraudulently obtain money from ill-informed academics looking for a place to publish their work.
551.	Predict and control	The original objective of natural scientists was to be able to predict and control the environment in which the human race lived. The success of this endeavour led to science seeking to study human activity with the hope that similar results could be obtained. However,

No.	Term	Definition
		this has not been achieved to the same extent.
552.	Pre-field procedures	Before a researcher commences the collection of data it is necessary to identify appropriate informants, obtain ethics clearance etc. The research instrument also needs to be validated. All these are regarded and described as pre-field procedures.
553.	Premodern	Refers to the period in history during which knowledge was obtained by consulting oracles, shamans, the entrails of animals and holy texts. Superstitions play important role in such societies.
		In Europe knowledge was largely controlled by the Catholic Church whose interpretation of the Judeo-Christian holy books was considered as the primary source of knowledge. This period ended in Europe with the commencement of the enlightenment at approximately 1600 CE. Galileo, a leading figure in the enlightenment pointed out that the holy books told how to go to heaven and not how the heavens go.
		Through the application of the scientific method pre-modern societies developed knowledge and technology to become modern.
		The term can also be used to describe societies who live in remote parts of the

Glossary of Research Concepts and Issues

No.	Term	Definition
		world and who do not have the facilities provided by modern technology such as electricity or medicine.
554.	Presentation tools	A variety of software products which facilitate the clear communication of a research project's progress or findings and conclusions.
555.	Pre-test	Research instruments need to be tested. Traditionally a pilot test was performed but in recent years it has become customary to perform another test before the pilot study. This is a simpler test which is often referred to as a pre-test.
556.	Prima facie	Latin term meaning *at first sight*.
557.	Primary data	Data collected or acquired by the researcher him or herself. Before this activity, primary data will not have been analysed or published.
558.	Principal component analysis	A variation of factor analysis which seeks to establish correlations between variables in a multivariate model.
559.	Prizes	Academic researchers sometimes offer informants entry into a raffle for the prospect of winning a prize as a thank you gesture for supplying data. This practice is in general not highly regarded and may not be approved by an ethics committee.

Glossary of Research Concepts and Issues

No.	Term	Definition
560.	Pro tem	Latin abbreviation for the term pro tempore meaning *temporary* or *for now*.
561.	Probing	Sometimes an informant does not provide a satisfactory answer to a question put to him or her during an interview. When this occurs the researcher may rephrase the question and put it to the informant again. This process is referred to as probing. If the informant does not want to answer the question no amount of probing will help and it may cause tension between the researcher and the informant. Thus probing should be used with caution.
562.	Process mapping	In the academic research context process mapping is a diagrammatic presentation of the activities required to conduct competent academic research.
563.	Professional doctorate	A doctoral degree which has a specific professional orientation, such as a Doctor of Business Administration (DBA) or a Doctor of Engineering (D Eng) to mention only two examples. There are many professional doctorates offered today in a wide range of subject areas and these are intended to help individuals to achieve both academic and professional excellence. These degrees are sometimes referred to as Prof Docs. Professional doctorates are sometimes not as well regarded in academe as the

Glossary of Research Concepts and Issues

No.	Term	Definition
		traditional PhD but they are sometimes preferred by non-academic employers.
564.	Professional journal	A publication which has not been produced for the academic community and in which the articles will not normally be peer reviewed and thus will not be considered as trustworthy or valuable as those which appear in an academic journal. Articles or papers in an academic journal will normally be double blind peer reviewed. Traditionally a professional journal was not considered as an appropriate source of information for a literature review.
565.	Professor Sir Cyril Burt	A research fraudster who claimed to have conducted a substantial amount of research leading to the conclusion that it would be beneficial for children to be tested for intellectual ability at the age of approximately 11 years. This led to the streaming of children into either an academic based education or a skill/trade type of education. It was eventually discovered that Burt had not done the research he claimed to have done and that he had no research evidence to support his educational claims.
566.	Promotor	See Research Supervisor
567.	Proof	A proof is a claim for the acceptance of an idea or a proposition to be correct or true. It is a term used by

No.	Term	Definition
		mathematicians and some other specialised professionals to support their claim that a statement is correct. Either evidence or arguments are normally offered to support the claim of proof. In the academic world the problem with the concept of proof originates from the difficulty in knowing if all the appropriate evidence on the subject is available and has been appropriately considered. The word proof should be used with considerable caution by academics in general.
568.	Proof Reading	The detailed examination of a piece of text in order to eliminate as many typographical or spelling errors as possible. A proof reader need not be an expert in the field of study but will probably be a native speaker of the language in question.
569.	Proposal	A document developed by a prospective research degree candidate in order to demonstrate that he or she has an understanding of the key issues within the field of study which is being considered.
		Most universities require a research proposal before formal registration for a degree takes place. Some universities require a modest document of perhaps 10 to 20 pages. Others demand an extensive piece of work, perhaps involving a substantial literature review and some

Glossary of Research Concepts and Issues

No.	Term	Definition
		preliminary work of possible sources of data. This could require a document of 100 pages.
570.	Proposition	The term proposition is in some respects a synonym for hypothesis. However, the term proposition is more commonly used by qualitative researchers and hypothesis is generally used by quantitative researchers. See *Hypothesis*
571.	Protocol	Rules or guidelines which direct the processes of the research project.
572.	Proving a hypothesis	A common mistake made sometimes by newcomers to academic research is to assert that a hypothesis has been proven to be correct. This is not an acceptable interpretation of the outcome of hypothesis testing. Hypotheses are tested for the purpose of their being rejected. If the researcher does not have the data to reject the hypotheses then the finding of the research is correctly stated as "the hypotheses have not been rejected". When this occurs, it can be argued that the hypotheses may be accepted pro tem i.e. for the time being.
573.	Pseudoscience	Explanations of phenomena which are not based on sound scientific thinking and practice and which are not

Glossary of Research Concepts and Issues

No.	Term	Definition
		accepted by the scientific community. This term is essentially pejorative.
574.	Public examination	In some parts of continental Europe the viva voce examination of doctoral candidates is normally held in public, i.e. in front of an uninvited audience. The definition of public varies in that in some places anyone may attend and question the degree candidate while in other countries the candidates may only be questioned by those who already have a doctorate and who submit their question in writing 24 hours in advance. The viva voce examination in English speaking countries is held in private.
575.	Publish or perish	A term dating from the first half of the 20th century which describes the pressure exerted on academics to have their research work published in peer reviewed academic journals. In many universities a publishing record is a prerequisite for an appointment as a faculty member. Universities often have rules regarding the number of papers an academic should publish on a regular basis. Today it is important for academics to have their work published in what are regarded as high-quality peer reviewed academic journals.
576.	Publishing	In the academic environment publishing mostly refers to research being

Glossary of Research Concepts and Issues

No.	Term	Definition
		accepted and included in peer reviewed scientific journals.
		Academics may also have their work published in books which are often referred to as monographs.
		Academics do not obtain any professional kudos for having textbooks published in their name. This activity is perceived to be strictly for money making purposes.
577.	Pure research	Similar to basic research or fundamental research the term pure research is used to indicate research which may not have any direct or immediate application.
578.	Purposeful Sampling	Any one of several sampling techniques which has a specific objective or data requirement in mind. In a sense all sampling is purposeful, but this term is normally used when a type of non-random sampling is to be employed.
579.	Puzzle solving	Routine research practice which does not lead to any interesting findings which could change our perception of the topic being researched. It has been argued that most academic research falls into this category. See *Scientific revolution*

Glossary of Research Concepts and Issues

Qual to Questionnaire protocol

No.	Term	Definition
580.	Qual	Abbreviated or shortened form of qualitative.
581.	Qualitative Comparative Analysis (QCA)	Originally developed by Charles Ragin in 1987 it is a data analysis technique for determining which logical conclusions a data set supports.
582.	Qualitative research	Research which primarily uses words and images as the primary data source. Some numeric data such as tables and graphs may be used without changing its status as qualitative research.
583.	Quant	Abbreviated or shortened form of quantitative.
584.	Quantitative research	An approach to research which is primarily based on the acquisition of numeric data and the analysis thereof with mathematical or statistical tools.
585.	Quasi-experimental	An experimental activity which does not fully comply with the rigor required for a scientific experiment. The difference between the scientific experiment and

No.	Term	Definition
		the quasi-experiment may take a number of forms one of which is that in a quasi-experiment the participants will not have been randomly selected. http://writing.colostate.edu/guides/research/glossary/
586.	Questionnaire	A data collection device which normally collects quantitative data but may also be used to obtain limited amounts of qualitative data.
587.	Questionnaire protocol	The rules under which a questionnaire is created, administered and analysed as part of an academic research project.

Radical scepticism to Role playing

No.	Term	Definition
588.	Radical scepticism	A philosophical stance which argues that any knowledge may actually be impossible. Although this position may be logically possible, it is of no practical value to academic researchers.
		However, all academic research is based on a more moderate form of scepticism which requires a researcher not to accept any proposition without enquiring as to the evidence on which the proposition was based.
589.	Random	Something is said to have the characteristic of randomness if it has a lack of pattern or predictability about it.
		Randomness is an important aspect of sample selection when using inferential statistics. A random sample is normally required and the characteristic of this sample is that any element of the population could have been chosen for inclusion in the sample.

Glossary of Research Concepts and Issues

No.	Term	Definition
590.	Random sample	A sample chosen in such a way that there is no relationship between the data elements which have been selected other than chance. It is in practice difficult to create a random sample.
591.	Randomised control group	Experimental science requires researchers to compare the results of an intervention with what happens if there is no intervention.
		Thus, in testing a drug there needs to be one group to whom the drug is administered and another group to whom a placebo is provided.
		The group to whom the placebo is administered is referred to as the control group.
		In such experiments it is important that there is no bias present in the way the control group is chosen and therefore choosing individuals at random is regarded as the most satisfactory way of assembling such a group. Such a group is referred to as a Randomised control group.
		http://en.wikipedia.org/wiki/Randomized_controlled_trial
592.	Range	The difference between the highest value and the lowest value in a data set. It is a simple measure of the dispersion in a data set.

Glossary of Research Concepts and Issues

No.	Term	Definition
593.	Ratio data	Data that indicates both magnitude and degree of magnitude so that the differences between them and their ratios are apparent. An example would be the size of different cities. City A has 2 million people, City B has 4 million people and City C has 8 million people. Thus, city C is twice the size of city B and four times the size of city A.
594.	Rationalism	An approach to understanding the world based on the paramount importance of reason or logic as the driver of understanding. This stance asserts that thinking is more important than observation. Those who advocate rationalism regard it as superior to empiricism because of the possibility of our senses being deceived. Rationalists argue that it is more difficult to deceive the mind than the eye and the other senses. htp://plato.stanford.edu/entries/rationalism-empiricism/
595.	Raw data	A term used to describe data before any processing has been attempted.
596.	Readability	The degree to which a piece of text can be easily read and understood. It is a function of the length of sentences used and the number of complex words employed. Clarity and simplicity are important dimensions of readability.

Glossary of Research Concepts and Issues

No.	Term	Definition
		Expressing ideas simply is a positive attribute to which academic researchers should aspire but it is possible to over simplify explanation and thus dumb down the subject. This is described as presenting the work at a simplistic level and has little or no academic merit. Academic text should be clear but not expressed in too simplistic terms. http://en.wikipedia.org/wiki/Readability
597.	Realism	A philosophical position which takes the view that there exists a real objective world independent of our perception of it and that this world can be known in the same way to all those who wish to be aware of it. Realism should be contrasted with relativism which asserts that each individual experiences the world differently. There are several categories within the realm of realism.
598.	Reason	An aspect of the employment of the mind to problem solving. The word reason overlaps to an extent with rationality or rationalism. It refers to the application of logic to an understanding of the world.
599.	Re-coding	Coding is an important tool for the organisation of data in order to understand its potential meaning. Sometimes codes are chosen in advance of the

Glossary of Research Concepts and Issues

No.	Term	Definition
		coding exercise and sometimes after a coding exercise the researcher reconsiders the situation and comes to the conclusion that other codes would have been more appropriate. If this occurs the data may need to be re-coded.
		The term re-coding may also be used in a different context. Coding is recognised as being a subjective process. In order to satisfy themselves that the coding has been performed correctly some researchers will have another individual re-code the data. Any differences in the coding can then be examined and adjustments made if necessary.
600.	Recording	This term is usually applied to capturing electronically the details of an event. This amounts to making an audio or a video recording of some research activity such as an interview, a focus group or some other situation of interest. Ethics committee permission is normally required before any recording can take place, as well as gaining consent from the research participants.
601.	Reddit	Reddit describes itself as a social news aggregation, web content rating, and discussion website.
602.	Reductionism	Reducing a research problem or question to a number of smaller problems or questions which may be solved or answered one at a time. This has also

Glossary of Research Concepts and Issues

No.	Term	Definition
		sometimes been referred to as atomism. Reductionism is one of the more important drivers of the success of the scientific method as experienced in modernism.
		Issues related to the experience of people as individuals, groups or organisations cannot easily be dissected in this fashion and often need to be studied holistically.
603.	Refereed publication	In order for academic output to be considered valuable it has to be evaluated by other academics of standing in the community.
		The process by which the work is evaluated is referred to as a review and reviewed work may be published in a refereed publication.
604.	Reference list	A list of sources of authority which have been cited in a piece of academic writing.
		A reference list is not a bibliography.
605.	Referencing	The use of an indicator which allows a reader to locate, in order to consult, the original source of a paper or a book which has been referred to in a piece of academic work.
		There are a number of different referencing systems used which include:-

Glossary of Research Concepts and Issues

No.	Term	Definition
		- Modern Humanities Research Association (MHRA),
- The Harvard System (often called the 'Author Date System'),
- Chicago System,
- Modern Language Association of America (MLA),
- American Psychological Association (APA).

http://www.bristol.ac.uk/arts/exercises/referencing/referencing%20skills/page_05.htm |
| 606. | Reflection | The process of introspection by the researcher on various aspects of the research such as what do the results of the research actually mean. Reflection is also used to explore the motives of the researcher and the choices which have been made during the research process. Researchers sometimes reflect on the future use of their findings although in general it is sometimes said that not enough attention is given to this aspect of research. |
| 607. | Reflective equilibrium | After a period of reflection it is hoped that the researcher will have a better understanding of what he or she has been doing and why it has been done. This reflection may lead to a feeling of having arrived at a better level of appreciation of the research processes and |

No.	Term	Definition
		what can be argued to have been achieved by the research. http://plato.stanford.edu/entries/reflective-equilibrium/
608.	Reflexive/ Reflexivity	The word reflexive is used to describe a deeper level of reflection which explores the motives of the researcher as well as his or her values and how these are expressed in terms of the subject of the research, methodologies used and the findings established.
609.	Registration	A formal act by which an individual is accepted by the university. The term is also used to describe the process of being formally accepted by the faculty or the department for a course of study or for a research degree. An adequate level of previous intellectual achievement has normally to be demonstrated for such acceptance by the university. See *Enrolment*
610.	Regression towards the mean	A principle in statistics and logic which states that if a sample is taken which appears to have an unusually high mean, then a second sample will probably show a lower mean. This principle applies to many aspects of life.

Glossary of Research Concepts and Issues

No.	Term	Definition
611.	Regression analysis	A statistical modelling approach which describes the relationship between two or more variables.
612.	Relativism	A philosophical stance which argues that there is no objective way of knowing or understanding the world. Each individual has a point of view which directly affects how he or she understands the world. The point of view is a function of history, culture, personal characteristics, family and aspirations. Sometimes this is described as each individual having his or her own reality, although it may be clearer to say that each person has their personal lens through which the world is understood. Taken to an extreme, relativism suggests that there can be little understanding between individuals or groups because of the different perspectives they hold. Clearly this is not true because despite any differences humans have much in common. http://plato.stanford.edu/entries/relativism/
613.	Relevant	Being of some importance to an audience or group of stakeholders. Academic research will normally need to have some practical value in use before it may be considered as relevant.

Glossary of Research Concepts and Issues

No.	Term	Definition
614.	Reliability	Whether the research can be repeated elsewhere with the same results. This is of considerable importance in positivistic research. Because of the general lack of control interpretivist research does not argue that a high degree of reliability can be achieved in the same way as quantitative research does. There are several different forms of reliability. http://bit.ly/1vj9qrt
615.	Remote Interviewing	The use of a videoconferencing product to conduct a research interview. This was previously thought to be inferior to a face-to-face encounter with an informant but due to the circumstances brought about by Covid-19, it is now completely accepted.
616.	Replication	Repeating an experiment to demonstrate its validity and reliability. Replication is a crucial aspect of the physical and life sciences. In the social sciences replication is not always possible.
617.	Representative realism	The world as it is cannot be directly perceived. But it is possible to perceive impressions of the world which say a substantial amount about it and which can be used to know the world. This is the modern equivalent of Plato and the parable of the Cave.

Glossary of Research Concepts and Issues

No.	Term	Definition
618.	Representative sampling	The statistical techniques available in quantitative research are based on the notion that a researcher can obtain random samples when acquiring data. It is difficult to achieve this and so in practice representative samples are often used as a surrogate for a random sample. There is some controversy as to the acceptability of this practice.
619.	Republic of scholars	A term use to suggest that there is an egalitarian attitude among academics to issues related to scholarship. This is based on the notion that it is the argument or the science which counts and not the person who has made it. In practice this is seldom the case.
620.	Research	An intellectual activity in which a question is attempted to be answered. Academic research follows to some extent a formal procedure including the formulation of a research question, usually accompanied by sub-questions, the establishment of a research design, the collection of data or evidence, the analysis of the data and the reaching of a conclusion as a result thereof. There is a high degree of flexibility as to how these processes are actually performed.
621.	Research advisor	A term sometimes used as a synonym for research supervisor. In continental Europe the term research promoter is

No.	Term	Definition
		used to describe the person who looks after and assists the research degree candidate.
622.	Research concept note	A structured approach to commencing a research project. The research concept note addresses the major issues which need to be explored before a research proposal can be written.
623.	Research governance	The rules laid down by the university or community or the national or local government under which the research needs to be conducted. Research governance focuses on appropriate practice which will comply with the required level of ethical behaviour.
624.	Research network	Research used to be envisaged as an activity conducted by a lone researcher on his or her own. There were many examples of this in former times. However today it is recognized that the research prospers by the application of different minds and different eyes. Researchers are now encouraged to form groups of people with whom they can share ideas and even collaborate. Such a group is referred to as a research network. There are many internet-based products and services which can facilitate online research networking.
625.	Research objective	What the researcher wishes to achieve as a result of the research. The term

No.	Term	Definition
		research objective is sometimes used in place of research question although in the academic research environment it is usually thought that research question is preferable.
626.	Research problem	Academic research especially in the social sciences is usually driven by an attempt to answer a research question. The research question is normally one aspect of a greater research problem which lies behind the issues being studied.
627.	Research process	The list of activities which need to be accomplished if creditable research is to be performed.
628.	Research proposal	See *Proposal*
629.	Research protocol	A document outlining how the research will be conducted. This is an important planning tool which needs to address a number of different issues concerning the research procedures. A research protocol will sometimes be produced as part of a research proposal.
630.	Research question	This is the raison d'être of the research. The researcher tries to find an answer to the research question. Without a research question academic research has no direction and it may even be regarded as not being research at all.

Glossary of Research Concepts and Issues

No.	Term	Definition
631.	Research tradition	Research may be conducted in many different ways and researchers often argue for the superiority of their chosen approach.
632.	Research and development (R&D)	A term used to describe research and its application which is conducted in a non-academic environment such as business or government.
633.	Research assistants	Research degree candidates may obtain assistance with some minor aspects of their research from research assistants. Such help needs to be limited to routine aspects of the work in order to be acceptable for an academic degree.
634.	Research associate	A term which is sometimes used to refer to research degree candidates in place of research student.
635.	Research audit	An investigation into the details of the work reported in a dissertation. A detailed record of the research activities should be kept by the researcher. The research diary may be useful in this respect.
636.	Research chair	A professorial position where the main activity of the incumbent is to conduct and publish his or her research. Some teaching may be required but by far the strongest emphasis of such an appointment is the publishing of research.
637.	Research concept note	A preliminary statement which attempts to outline the main issues

Glossary of Research Concepts and Issues

No.	Term	Definition
		involved in a proposed academic research project. A research concept note will address inter alia a working title, a review of which sources of academic literature will be most likely to be useful, and the type of data which should be acquired.
		The research concept note is a document which can be used to explore the viability of a research project as well as to make some initial plans as to how to commence the project.
638.	Research degree examination	Research degrees are examined in different ways in different countries. However, the decision to award the degree is at the discretion of the University Senate. The University Senate will normally delegate this authority to a committee which may be referred to as the examinations board or higher degree committee or some such title. The decision is taken on the basis of reports received from examiners.
		In general, the completed dissertation is formally examined often by both internal and external examiners. In some countries the examiners write reports and this is all that is required. In other countries the examiners' reports are only part of the process which demands the degree candidate to face a panel and orally defend his or her work. In

Glossary of Research Concepts and Issues

No.	Term	Definition
		some countries this is referred to as a viva voce and in North America, the defence.
		In certain Europe countries the defence is held in front of a public audience while in the United Kingdom it is conducted in private.
639.	Research design	Either the process of producing a research plan or the finished product of a statement describing how the research is intended to be conducted.
640.	Research diary	By making regular entries a research diary allows the researcher to keep an audit trail of his/her research activities as well as an account of how the researcher's thinking develops over the period of the research.
		The term research log is also used.
		http://bit.ly/1qK2Inp
641.	Research education	Research degrees traditionally relied on the apprenticeship model whereby the degree candidate worked closely with an accomplished practitioner i.e. the supervisor. This model meant that the research degree candidate had very little contact with anyone else in the university. The result of this process has been criticised as producing scholars with a narrow view of research and its place in the academic world.

Glossary of Research Concepts and Issues

No.	Term	Definition
		Today most research degree candidates are required to attend a range of seminars or courses in different aspects of research philosophy, research design, analytical tools to mention only a few issues. This is referred to as research education as well as the delivery of transferable skills.
		See *Transferable skills*
642.	Research involving patients	If a research project involves the study of anyone who is receiving medical treatment or it involves how such people are treated by doctors, hospital or the health service, it may need additional ethics approval from the National Health Service.
643.	Research log	See *Research diary*
644.	Research memo	A term used in the Grounded Theory Method to describe notes created by a researcher during the processes of research and which should be incorporated into whatever transcripts are being produced for further analysis.
645.	Research panel	A group of people who have been selected as informants for the purposes of conducting opinion-based research.
		Most often a research panel will be designed to represent a population of interest. Thus, they may consist of a group with a particular demographic quality or they may be consumers of a

Glossary of Research Concepts and Issues

No.	Term	Definition
		particular type of product or something similar.
		Panels are more appropriate for commercial research than for academic research
646.	Research philosophy	Every research tactic has a philosophical underpinning. For example, whether a research takes a quantitative or a qualitative path to understanding and answering the research question reflects his or her view on how society should be understood. There are a large range of philosophical stances and it is important for researchers to understand the options which are available in this respect.
647.	Research risk	The possibility that the research might fail, i.e. not achieve the objectives of the research.
648.	Researcher assumptions	The key assumptions which underpin academic research include: • the world is understandable; • we want to understand the world about us; • we have an open minded approach to the research; • the researcher is capable of objective reasoning; • we can seldom if ever incorporate in our research all the issues or

Glossary of Research Concepts and Issues

No.	Term	Definition
		variables concerned with the phenomenon we are studying; • a simple model of reality may sometimes provide more understanding then a complex one; • our cognitive capacity is limited and changes over time; • it cannot be said that our findings or the theory produced there from are indisputably correct.
649.	Researcher safety	One of the issues which ethics committees consider is the risk of harm coming to the researcher as a result of the research project. Ethics committees would oppose any proposal which might cause the researcher to be exposed to any situation which could lead to physical or emotional harm.
650.	Researcher values	The key values which drive academic research are a belief in the importance of creating new knowledge and a desire to share any knowledge created with the greater community.
651.	Research report	This term is often used as a synonym for mini-dissertation. See *Mini-dissertation*.
652.	Residence requirements	Some universities require their degree candidates to live within a given distance of the university. If they do not reside nearby they may not be enrolled. This condition is increasingly being relaxed.

Glossary of Research Concepts and Issues

No.	Term	Definition
653.	Respect	Researchers will often encounter a wide range of informants of varying quality. It is important that the researcher affords a high level of respect to all those who make any contribution to the research activity.
654.	Re-submission	After examination a dissertation frequently requires corrections, changes, modification or improvements. When this is completed the dissertation needs to be resubmitted for final approval and acceptance.
655.	Retrospective ethics applications	In general ethics committees are opposed to granting approval for research projects which have already begun or that are completed. Many universities now insist that all research projects including all research degree activities have ethics committee approval. Sometimes administrative mistakes are made and projects do begin before approval is granted. In such cases exceptions are sometimes made and retrospective approval is given.
656.	Reviewer confidentiality	It customary for many journals that the identity of reviewers are not disclosed. In some cases the reviewer's identity is disclosed when the paper has been accepted for publication.

Glossary of Research Concepts and Issues

No.	Term	Definition
657.	Reviews	Comments supplied by individuals who have been asked to examine a proposed academic paper submitted to a journal.
658.	Revisions	Examiners may require research dissertations to be revised to remove errors or to improve the work presented. There are normally two distinct categories of revisions which are minor and major revisions.
659.	Rhetoric	A rather old-fashioned word whose meaning has somewhat changed over time. Rhetoric was simply a synonym for argument. However today it often has a negative connotation implying that it is in some way a false argument.
660.	Rich description	A thoroughly detailed account of the phenomenon. This term implies that a considerable amount of time has been spent in order to really understand and describe the phenomenon being addressed. See *Thick description*
661.	Right to withdraw	Research governance requires researchers to offer research participants the right to withdraw from any experiment or survey at any time without having to justify such withdrawal.
662.	Rigor	Strictly complying with the rules of a particular research paradigm. There are

Glossary of Research Concepts and Issues

No.	Term	Definition
		several different ways in which rigor can be applied to a research project.
663.	Risk	The concept of risk relates to the fact that there is always the possibility that what is envisaged by planners may not occur. So, if it is envisaged that a research project will take two years there is the risk that due to unforeseen issues it may take longer or it may not be possible to complete the project at all.
664.	Risk assessment	A risk assessment makes an evaluation of the likelihood of problems arising during the research.
665.	Robust findings	Research findings which have been produced through a rigorous approach to the research.
666.	Role playing	A simulation exercise whereby individuals behave as if they had a particular function. For example, asking students to make decisions about investments which would normally be made by managers. See *Surrogates*

Sample to Systematic literature review

No.	Term	Definition
667.	Sample	A subset of the population which is being studied. There are a number of different ways of designing a sample.
668.	Sample frame	The group of data from which the sample is selected. It is a list or working subset of the population.
669.	Sample size	The number of data points used in the calculations. Different statistical techniques require different sample sizes and it is important to know the sample size required before commencing data collection.
670.	Scatter diagram	Normally a two-dimensional graphical representation of data displayed in terms of an X and a Y co-ordinate. Scatter diagrams are created so that a researcher can eyeball the data to ascertain if there might be any patterns i.e. any apparent relationship between the variables.

Glossary of Research Concepts and Issues

No.	Term	Definition
671.	Scatter diagram	Normally reserved for 2 dimensional graphs consisting of X and Y-axes. A diagram showing the location of data points on an axis without any joining lines.
672.	Scepticism	An attitude of doubt whereby the researcher seeks evidence to support any claim being made before accepting its possible correctness. Academic research is based on the principle that no claim should be accepted unless adequate evidence is supplied in support of the claim.
673.	Schism	Schism is used to describe a break or parting between two previously united individuals. The word schism is often used to describe division in churches. In research methodology the differences of opinion concerning the Grounded Theory Method by its proponents Glaser and Strauss have been described as a schism.
674.	Scholarly journal	A journal which publishes double blind peer reviewed papers reporting on academic research of interest to the community of scholars.
675.	Scholarship	A characteristic involving being well read and also being able to use such knowledge to create convincing arguments in the scholar's field of interest. Scholarship requires the ability to critique as well as assemble new concepts

Glossary of Research Concepts and Issues

No.	Term	Definition
		and skilfully present them to peers for review and comment.
676.	Scholarship - Money	Monies made available to support normally impecunious students with their fees and other expenses. Scholarships are normally awarded for superior past academic performance. There is normally no condition attached to the awarding of a scholarship. See *Bursary*
677.	Science	Based on the Latin word *scio* which means to know, science may be described as the process of adding something of value to the body of theoretical knowledge. Carefully following this process is regarded as taking a rigorous approach to research. It is usually argued that through science that we can formally claim to know or to have knowledge. It is also argued by others that there are different types of knowledge some of which have no connection to science. This leads into a discussion of epistemological issues and the values of researchers.
678.	Scientific community	There are many different scientific communities. Each field of study will have its own community. The community consists of scholars who are attempting to or who have already made a

Glossary of Research Concepts and Issues

No.	Term	Definition
		contribution to the body of knowledge in that field of study. Scientific communities are normally found at universities, research institutes or other centres of learning.
679.	Scientific research	Research conducted in such a way that it is deemed acceptable by the scientific community. It should be contrasted with commercial research which attempts to solve a business problem without concern for any other degree of acceptability. Scientific research will have a number of characteristics which will include:- • Acknowledgement of currently accepted knowledge of that topic through the literature review; • A critical or even sceptical outlook; • A careful articulation of the research question; • A well constructed research design.
680.	Scientific revolution	A term coined by Thomas Kuhn to describe how scientific progress sometimes occurs by abruptly overthrowing an older established theory or paradigm. This is to be contrasted with routine research/science which Kuhn referred to as puzzle solving. Kuhn coined the term paradigm shift which he claimed only happened through the process of a scientific revolution.

Glossary of Research Concepts and Issues

No.	Term	Definition
		http://www.youtube.com/watch?v=_Y-svkL6zdo
681.	Scientific method	A group of techniques which are used by researchers to answer questions which will lead to the addition of something of value to the body of knowledge. There is some debate as to which techniques should be regarded as being a part of the scientific method.
		Traditionally the term scientific method was reserved to describe laboratory research, but it is now understood that it is possible to be scientific in a number of different situations besides those found in a laboratory.
		http://www.youtube.com/watch?v=PrIl9oErJJg
		http://www.youtube.com/watch?v=XdRH552uytk
682.	Search engine	A software product which facilitates finding information on the web.
		There are many specialised search engines which can be of particular assistance to researchers.
683.	Secondary data	Data which has already been processed and published. This is contrasted with primary data which is directly collected or generated by the researcher him/herself.

Glossary of Research Concepts and Issues

No.	Term	Definition
684.	Second supervisor	It is increasingly popular for universities to appoint more than one supervisor for doctoral degree candidates. Two supervisors are often used but the role of the second supervisor can in some cases be quite minimal.
685.	Secularism	A belief that knowledge can be established by scientific processes without reference to any religious texts. This concept was important during the period referred to as the enlightenment when the power of the church to adjudicate what was acceptable knowledge first came into question.
686.	Self-completion questionnaires	A questionnaire which is designed to be completed by the informant without any help from the researcher. Most questionnaires used in academic research are self-completion questionnaires especially if they are administered electronically.
687.	Self-plagiarism	This refers to the use of material by the same author which has already been published elsewhere and which is being re-submitted for further publication without acknowledging its original publication.
688.	Self-publishing	It is increasingly acceptable for a researcher to take the necessary steps to publish, on their own, his or her dissertation as a monograph. There are now

Glossary of Research Concepts and Issues

No.	Term	Definition
		many agencies who will arrange for a book to be produced.
689.	Self-report studies	These are research studies in which the researcher reports on how he or she reacted to a particular situation or phenomenon.
		There is always an element of self-reporting in a study where field notes are involved as these are often if not usually reports on how the researcher experienced his or her encounter with another research participant or informant.
690.	Semi-structured interview	An interview which is based around a series of issues on which the researcher asks the informant to supply information, comments or remarks. A semi-structured interview normally employs an interview schedule which is a list of issues to be discussed. The researcher will normally pose these issues in the form of open-ended questions.
691.	Senior doctorates	A doctoral degree awarded by universities in recognition of the lifelong work of an individual. No dissertation is presented for such a degree but rather a copy of all the work ever published by the person being considered for this award.
692.	Sensed data	The result of directly observing a phenomenon of interest to the researcher. Empirical research is thought by

No.	Term	Definition
		extreme researchers to be wholly dependent on sense data and that the researcher has to observe the entities being researched. If this were true then atomic physics and other branches of science which look at invisible entities would not be counted as research.
693.	Sensitivity analysis	A technique used in mathematical analysis to explore the relative importance of different variables in a model.
694.	Sent down	This term is used as a euphemism for being expelled from the university. Research degree candidates could be sent down for gross misconduct which would normally mean some criminal behaviour or perhaps some form of academic cheating. Oxford, Cambridge and Durham use the term rustication instead.
695.	Sentiment analysis	A technique used with big data sets to draw a conclusion about the general feeling or mood expressed in a large set of comments.
696.	Serendipity	The notion of serendipity normally arises in respect of the researcher encountering additional and unexpected sources of data. This may become problematical if the Ethics Committee believes that this data is outside the scope of the Ethics Protocol.

Glossary of Research Concepts and Issues

No.	Term	Definition
697.	Simplistic	The characteristic of presenting information in an over simplified way and thereby detracting from its value.
		A more modern way of describing this phenomenon is *dumbing down*.
698.	Simulation	A simulation is a representation of the operation of an entity or a phenomenon in order to be able to acquire a better understanding of its functioning or characteristics.
		Simulation normally involves the building of a model which is then tested in some way. Examples of this would be a model aircraft tested in a wind tunnel or a business model tested in a computer using some form of what-if analysis.
699.	Single blind reviewing	When the reviewer knows the identity of the author being reviewed but not vice versa.
700.	Single case study research	A question which is continually being asked is: "How many case studies are needed for a research degree, especially a doctorate?"
		There is no simple answer to this as it depends upon many different issues. However, it is perfectly possible to obtain a doctorate having only studied one single case. In general, there will have

Glossary of Research Concepts and Issues

No.	Term	Definition
		to be a special reason why only one case study was used.
701.	Situating the perspective of the researcher	The term 'situating the perspective' of the researcher is used in qualitative research and suggests that the researcher should explain the philosophical underpinning and values of the researcher when reporting the findings.
702.	Snowballing	A sampling technique which requires the researcher to seek the identity of suitable knowledgeable informants from individuals who have previously provided information to the researcher.
703.	Social constructivism	A view that understanding and knowledge are the product of the individual's and the society's values in which they are created. Social constructivism is based on an ontological stance which emphases relativism. http://www.youtube.com/watch?v=GVVWmZAStn8 http://www.youtube.com/watch?v=gBvHA6SwXSk&feature=fvw
704.	Social bookmarking	Software products which allow researchers to store and share web links with each other.
705.	Social desirability	Some research projects are considered socially desirable and other are not. Socially undesirable research would

Glossary of Research Concepts and Issues

No.	Term	Definition
		include ways and means of increasing the efficiency of illegal conduct.
706.	Social media	A term used to describe a range of software products and websites which aim to facilitate messaging and networking. This range of products has become dominated by large USA providers.
707.	Social Media Chinese	In response to the large USA corporations who currently own most social media, Chinese entrepreneurs have developed a number of products of their own which perform the same function. These include WeChat, Sina Weibo, Tencent, QQ and Xiao Hong Shu.
708.	Social Science	The study of people and organizations using a structured approach often referred to as a scientific framework or a scientific method. Social science is contrasted with physical science or life sciences which study aspects of the physical world (physical science) or life processes (life sciences). Social science may also be contrasted with the study of the humanities which takes a more descriptive, critical and speculative approach to human subjects. Social science, physical science and life sciences often employ empirical methods which are less appropriate in the humanities.

Glossary of Research Concepts and Issues

No.	Term	Definition
		http://www.youtube.com/watch?v=XkGe7PfsgMw
		http://www.youtube.com/watch?v=_EZcpTTjjXY
709.	Social software	Communication tools and interactive systems which may be used to facilitate networking between researchers.
710.	Sociogram	A diagram displaying the relationship between variables in order to make more obvious patterns and relationships which might not otherwise be visible.
711.	Sociology	The study of human behaviour in groups.
712.	Sociology of research	The study of how research is conducted in society. It addresses a wide range of issues of which academic research is only part.
713.	Sociology of research	The study of matters related to the environment in which academic research exists.
714.	Soft data	This is often used as a pejorative term to describe evidence which is not focused on numeric data. Qualitative research would generally focus on or employ soft data. See *Hard Data*
715.	Sound argument	See *Valid argument*

Glossary of Research Concepts and Issues

No.	Term	Definition
716.	Spinbot	A software product which will rewrite a piece of text so that the meaning is retained but the new text will appear to be an original piece of work.
717.	Sponsored research	Research for which the researcher or the university has received money or other resources.
		Research may be sponsored by an organisation offering a scholarship to a student or it could be funded less directly by money being paid to the university or the faculty or the school.
		Academic institutions mostly welcome sponsored research although there may be problems depending on the nature of the sponsor and their objectives.
718.	SPSS	SPSS stands for Statistical Package for the Social Sciences and has been in use since at least 1970. It is the leading software package for statistical analysis in the social sciences. It has been the mainstay of quantitative academic research for many decades.
719.	Spurious accuracy	A level of accuracy which is greater than that which has any value. Thus, to say that the average weight of the member of a class is 82.456 Kilograms would quite likely be spurious.
720.	Stakeholders	Those individuals and groups who have a direct interest in the research and its findings/conclusions. This includes the

Glossary of Research Concepts and Issues

No.	Term	Definition
		researcher, the supervisor, the university, the profession, other researchers, and potential examiners, to mention only a few possible stakeholders.
721.	Standardised measuring instruments	A measuring instrument which had been validated through some process of testing and is regarded as performing the function which is attributed to it.
722.	Standing on the shoulders of giants	This expression is often attributed to Isaac Newton when pointing to the large contribution of scientific discovery made by his forebearers. Today the expression maybe used to emphasise that any academic research project is required to have become familiar with the already published literature related to the topic.
723.	Statistical tests	Statistical tests are associated with hypothesis testing through the use of standard statistical techniques.
724.	Statistics	The term has two different meanings. Statistics may be facts, usually figures, about a situation such as the statistics for the football season for the local club were 12 wins and 10 lost matches. Statistics is also the art and the science of understanding data especially in respect of its inherent variability. It is this second meaning which is normally

No.	Term	Definition
		attributed to the word statistics in academic research.
725.	Steward of the discipline	A term used by the Carnegie Foundation's work on doctoral education to suggest that a doctoral graduate should be able to defend the established knowledge in his/her field of study.
		The emphasis which is normally placed on doctoral education is the creating of new knowledge but here the scope is widened to include understanding and arguing for the validity of established knowledge.
726.	Stratified sampling	A method of acquiring a sample which represents a population that consists of a number of sub-groups. The stratified sample ensures that each sub-group is adequately represented in the overall sample.
727.	Strong argument	An argument where there is adequate evidence and the rationale for the conclusion is clear.
728.	Strong theory	Some of the characteristics of strong theory are:- • Strong theory includes a detailed and compelling argument which is grounded in clear evidence. • Strong theory often has a limited number of variables, simply or clearly stated relationships.

Glossary of Research Concepts and Issues

No.	Term	Definition
		• Explained logical reasoning supporting the causative argument is a clear feature. • Strong theory is sufficiently abstract to have some claim of generality. • Strong theory leads to well-motivated hypotheses.
729.	Structural equation modelling (SEM)	The application of advanced statistics for the purposes of testing and estimating causal relations using a combination of data and assumptions.
730.	Structured literature review	See *Systematic literature review*
731.	Structuration Theory	A social theory which expresses the view that social systems are primarily based on both the structure and the agents involved. Neither of these has primacy, but they interact to determine the outcome or the shape of the social system.
732.	Structured interview	This involves the soliciting of data/evidence from an informant by means of a formal instrument such as a questionnaire.
733.	Subjective	A view is subjective if it is formulated in the mind of the thinker without reference to external opinions or much reflection on the basis on which the view is created. A subjective view makes little

Glossary of Research Concepts and Issues

No.	Term	Definition
		or no accommodation for the views of others.
		All human views are ultimately subjective although some are more subjective than others.
		An extreme form is referred to as Subjectivism which asserts that the world is nothing more than the view of the thinker.
734.	Submission details	Every university has its own rules regarding how a dissertation should be submitted. Some universities require the dissertation to be bound in a hard cover while others require soft binding. Some universities require two copies while others require many more. The description of the work, which has to be placed on the cover of the dissertation, also varies considerably. Many universities will refuse to accept a dissertation if their rules have not been precisely followed.
735.	Subscription database	A database for which the researcher has to make a payment in order to obtain access.
736.	Substantive theory	A theory which is applicable to the institution or the individuals who were participants in the research process. This type of theory would not necessarily be generalisable to a larger population. It is regarded as the first step in producing a

No.	Term	Definition
		grounded theory. Once the substantive theory is in place then it may be further refined into a formal theory which will have greater scope and generalisability.
737.	Summative evaluation	A summative evaluation provides a judgement as to whether or not an activity or a person or some other entity has been performing satisfactorily. It may also state the level of satisfaction being achieved.
738.	Superstition	A belief which is not firmly based on empirical evidence. There can be an overlap with superstitions and informal traditional knowledge or folk wisdom. Thus, an apple a day keeps the doctor away can be seen to have some folk knowledge for the human need for vitamins. Walking under a ladder bringing bad luck could be seen as simply common sense as if there is a ladder then maybe there will be someone up the ladder working and he or she could drop something on the head of the person passing underneath. However, the idea that an itchy palm suggests the imminent arrival of money is unlikely to have any basis in reality.
739.	Supervision	Academic research has traditionally been learnt through an apprenticeship process whereby a novice learns by working alongside an accomplished practitioner.

Glossary of Research Concepts and Issues

No.	Term	Definition
		The work involved in helping the novice learn his or her craft (research is a craft skill) is referred to as supervision.
		The quality of supervision is notoriously varied and can range from outstanding to neglect and even abandonment.
740.	Supervisor	An academic who is assigned to guide, manage or direct the work of a student normally in respect of research activities.
		Traditionally one supervisor was allocated to one research degree candidate, but that practice has changed. In some universities there are now two supervisors one of whom is referred to as the First supervisor and the other as the Second supervisor. The manner in which the responsibility for the progress of the research degree candidate is shared will vary according to the method of working together devised by the supervisors and the student.
		Some universities have moved to a supervisory panel, committee or team whereby there will be even more supervisors available to the student.
741.	Supervisor confidentiality	Those supervising students' research are expected to be careful about mentioning its progress or its implication with others.

Glossary of Research Concepts and Issues

No.	Term	Definition
742.	Supervisory committee	A committee comprising a number of academics tasked with assisting a doctoral degree candidate in his or her endeavours to conduct their research, produce their dissertation and face their examination. They are used in lieu of a single or pair of supervisors.
743.	Surrogates	In certain circumstances it may be difficult if not impossible to obtain access to the most appropriate individuals whom the researcher would like to involve in his or her research. In such cases surrogates are sometimes used. An example of this is the use of students in decision-making processes involving group decision support systems. Students are also sometimes used in investment decision-making experiments.
744.	Survey	The collection of a material amount of data. This term is normally used in connection with the data obtained by the use of a questionnaire which has been completed by a relatively large number of people.
745.	Survey Monkey	An open-source software product for the development and dissemination of questionnaires.
746.	Syllogism	A syllogism or an Aristotelian syllogism is a simple logical construct of the form: major premise, minor premise, and then conclusion.

Glossary of Research Concepts and Issues

No.	Term	Definition
		For example:
		Major premise - All cats have whiskers Minor premise - Tom has whiskers Conclusion - Tom is a cat.
		As may be seen the conclusion of a syllogism need not be logically correct.
		But
		Major premise - All cats have whiskers Minor premise - Tom is a cat Conclusion - Tom has whiskers.
747.	Symbolic Interactionism	Symbolic Interactionism is a sociological perspective which was coined by Herbert Blumer in Chicago in 1938 and its roots are traced back to ideas which are associated with American pragmatism. In this approach people are said to react to the meaning which acts or artefacts have for them and these actions are modified through social interaction and interpretation. http://web.grinnell.edu/courses/soc/s00/soc111-01/introtheories/symbolic.html
748.	Symmetrical interview	An interview whereby the interviewer and the informant share knowledge and ideas with each other on an equal or near equal basis. Such an interview may be described as a conversation between the researcher and the informant.

Glossary of Research Concepts and Issues

No.	Term	Definition
749.	Symposium	A meeting to discuss a subject, often an academic subject. The word is taken from the Greek where it is used to describe a drinking party.
750.	Syntax	The rules related to how to structure a sentence. It is a synonym for grammar.
751.	Systematic literature review	A review in which a body of literature is reviewed and assessed utilizing a pre-specified and standardized approach to reduce bias etc. As with a traditional literature review, the goal is to identify, critically appraise, and summarize the existing evidence concerning a clearly defined issue.

Tabula rasa to Twitter

No.	Term	Definition
752.	Tabula rasa	Latin term meaning *clean slate*. It has been argued by some philosophers that the mind of a newly born infant is a tabula rasa.
		In the academic research context, a tabula rasa would be a situation in which no previous research had been done.
753.	Telephone interview	Due to the increasing challenge of travel and the cost associated therewith researchers have begun to conduct interviews over telephones. Although this is acceptable a telephone interview does not give the researcher the opportunity of experiencing nonverbal cues delivered by the informant.
		Nor may a telephone interview allow the researcher to fully appreciate the environmental context in which the informant may be working.

Glossary of Research Concepts and Issues

No.	Term	Definition
754.	Tension	Term relating to a state of discomfort which can arise between a researcher and informants during a data or evidence collection episode. An informant may not wish to answer a specific question or having answered it may regret having so done. Tension can also arise between informants during a focus group if they hold different views or display different values.
755.	Tenure	Certain universities offer their faculty an employment contract which ensures long term employment. Individuals who are awarded such contracts are said to be tenured.
756.	Test-Retest Reliability	Used to assess the consistency of a measure from one time to another.
757.	Textual analysis	Refers to the process of understanding the written word. Even where interviews have been involved in the collection of data the content of the interviews is usually reduced to writing and then the transcript is subjected to textual analysis.
758.	Theoretical conjecture	A theoretical statement or even a more complete theory which has yet to be tested. Researchers will normally create a theoretical conjecture which the research will test.

Glossary of Research Concepts and Issues

No.	Term	Definition
759.	Theoretical sensitivity	A term used in the Grounded Theory Method to refer to a researcher's ability to identify theoretical explanations for the phenomenon which is being studied. An individual who has a degree of theoretical sensitivity will be well versed in theories related to the topics being researched and will be able to relate the evidence being acquired to an explanatory framework which will be developed into a theory.
760.	Theoretical memos	The recording of the researcher's thoughts on the theoretical implications of the data being supplied by the informants. This is a characteristic of grounded theory. Theoretical memos should be made as soon as possible and should be cross-referenced to the research diary.
761.	Theoretical sampling	Theoretical sampling is a form of purposeful sampling. It is a Grounded Theory Method related concept by which researchers find suitable research cases/participants/organisations so as to move the grounded theory research forward. The purpose of this type of sampling is to strengthen the researcher's theoretical understanding. Theoretical sampling may be thought of as a sort of triangulation. http://bit.ly/1qpCZV1

No.	Term	Definition
762.	Theoretical saturation	When additional informants do not provide any new data or insights the point of theoretical saturation has been reached and there is no value in seeking additional informants. This can also be referred to as data saturation. http://jin-thoughts.blogspot.com/2008/03/theoretical-saturation.html
763.	Theory	The word theory has many meanings in a wide variety of contexts. In academic research a theory is an explanation of how variables interact and the consequences of their interaction. A theory will explain how a phenomenon works but will not necessarily explain why it works. Addressing theory is a fundamental requirement of academic research.
764.	Theory triangulation	The use of more than one theoretical lens to understand the phenomenon such as agency theory and transfer pricing and contingency theory.
765.	Theory building	Theory building involves taking different ideas and showing how they can be perceived or combined to produce a greater understanding of the situation. It is the creative element of academic research and every researcher will do this differently. The outcome of a theory building exercise is the

No.	Term	Definition
		establishment of a new theory or theoretical conjecture. Sometimes a model is produced which is accompanied by a theoretical explanation. In this context the word model or thesis is sometimes used as a synonym for theory.
766.	Thesaurus	A collection of synonyms.
767.	Thesis	This word is used in two different ways. It can refer to the theoretical contribution of a piece of academic research and it can also be used to describe the book which is produced by the research as the final output of the work.
768.	Thick descriptions	Detailed in-depth descriptions which may be used to understand the situation and thus be an important factor in answering a research question. See *Rich description*
769.	Think aloud methods	See *Thought experiments*
770.	Thought experiment	This refers to the use of the imagination to envisage an experiment. The experiment may be one that could be enacted if the resources are available or it could be one which is simply hypothetical as in Schrödinger's cat, which illustrates quantum indeterminacy. Einstein claimed to have developed his theory of special relativity by imagining what it would be like to travel on a light wave.

No.	Term	Definition
		A thought experiment is a most important aspect of academic research.
771.	Threats to validity	A project's validity may be suspect for a number of reasons. The internal validity may be undermined by a lack of clarity in the expression of the research question. Problems may arise with regard to the integrity of the data or with the way the data has been managed or analysed or interpreted.
		External validity on the other hand may be threatened by issues related to the sample studied and to the extent that it was random or at least a good representative of the population of interest.
		http://pages.bangor.ac.uk/~pes004/resmeth/design/validmain.htm
772.	Time line research	Research which has as its main focus the timeframe in which events took place. This type of research may also be referred to as a chronology.
773.	Topology of design	Topology is the study of space, dimension and shape. Thus, topology of design refers to the overall characteristics of the research project. The topology of design of a project would describe at a high level the project's objectives, its general approach and the type of findings it is expected to produce.

Glossary of Research Concepts and Issues

No.	Term	Definition
774.	Transcript	A written record of the data/evidence/information supplied by informants or acquired from reports or other data sources. Most research projects require data of a number of different varieties and even data supplied as verbal responses needs, in general to be reduced to a transcript before it can be analysed, in any traditional meaning of the word analysed.
775.	Trans-disciplinary	Signifies a unity of knowledge beyond disciplines.
776.	Transfer process	Many universities do not allow direct registration for a doctoral degree. In these institutions degree candidates are initially registered for a master's degree although the intention is not necessarily to obtain a degree at this level. If good progress is made with the research then the degree candidate may ask to be considered to have his or her registration transferred from the master's degree register to the doctoral degree register. The process required for this would normally entail the production of a substantial piece of written work as well as a presentation at a seminar.
777.	Transferability	This is a qualitative research concept which is similar to the notion of generalisability in quantitative research. Transferability refers to the fact that the findings of some social science may be

Glossary of Research Concepts and Issues

No.	Term	Definition
		applicable to situations other than the one in which the research was conducted.
		Because qualitative researchers generally work with small samples, they are often concerned about whether their findings will be considered to be applicable in other situations or contexts. Quantitative researchers refer to this dimension of their research as its generalisabilty. Qualitative researchers use the term transferability.
778.	Transferable skills	Skills which may be used in a number of settings besides that of academic research. Thus, the ability to express oneself clearly and concisely in writing and the ability to create and verbally present complex ideas are considered transferable skills.
		The sophisticated use of statistics is frequently thought of as a transferable skill.
779.	Triangulation	Use of multiple lenses through which to consider the research question. There are several ways in which triangulation may be used such as data triangulation, informant triangulation, method triangulation, to mention only three. Triangulation uses multiple approaches or tools or data in order to obtain a greater understanding of the phenomenon being studied. Sometimes

Glossary of Research Concepts and Issues

No.	Term	Definition
		triangulation is seen as a method of cross-checking the credibility or validity of what is being discovered, but more correctly it offers a richer and more complete understanding of the phenomenon. Its cross-checking potential is strictly limited. http://searchnetworking.techtarget.com/sDefinition/0,,sid7_gci753924,00.html
780.	Trustworthiness	A concept used by qualitative researchers which in some ways straddles both the issues of validity and reliability. In this case more emphasis is given to what quantitative researchers refer to as validity.
781.	Truth	The word truth is problematic for many academic researchers in that it implies that there is one correct understanding of a situation or a concept. However, it is often the case that there are a number of ways of understanding what is or has been happening. Thus, there are often a number of different truths.
782.	Truth claims	Some researchers argue that the purpose of research is to make truth claims. In academic research a truth claim could be regarded as an assertion about the validity of a finding. However as there can be opposing truth claims

No.	Term	Definition
		this makes the use of this term problematic. http://www.youtube.com/watch?v=oL8MhYq9owo&feature=related
783.	Tutor	In a university environment a tutor is an individual who offers specific help with either academic affairs or with personal matters. Tutors are normally appointed by a specific department or school for one academic year at a time. Thus, there can be academic tutors and personal tutors.
784.	Twitter	A social media application with the primary purpose of connecting people by facilitating short messaging.

Unacceptable language to Useable returned questionnaire

No.	Term	Definition
785.	Unacceptable language	This issue arises mostly as a result of words used by informants during the taking of verbal evidence for example during interviews or focus groups. However, it can also occur with regard to writing accounts obtained by the researcher.
		In general expletives or derogatory or insulting words should not be recounted in academic discourse. These words are generally not acceptable. Euphemisms may sometimes be appropriate.
786.	Uncertainty	A concept which is similar to risk except whereas risk can sometimes be assessed to the point of quantification, uncertainty often cannot.
		The outcome of all research projects when considered in advance is at least to some degree uncertain.

No.	Term	Definition
787.	Unfamiliar journals	A journal which is not well known in the academic community. New journals will be unfamiliar to begin with and thus not all unfamiliar journals should be treated as predatory. Nonetheless there are an increasing number of predatory journals in circulation and academics should be careful of attempting to publish in journals which are not well known in their community.
788.	Unit of analysis	Academic research normally requires a high degree of focus in order to study the issues, entity, or phenomenon. This focus is placed on a unit of analysis which describes the point of interest of the research. The unit of analysis could be individuals, people, formal or informal groups, organisations, levels of investment, attitudes, performance levels or even national entities such as countries.
789.	Univariate analysis	Exploring how one variable affects one or more other variables.
790.	Unstructured interview	An interview during which the informant is asked to supply data on a topic without the researcher providing a structure as to how this data will be offered. The researcher asks the informant to comment on the topic of interest but does not intervene by asking specific questions or in any other way.

No.	Term	Definition
791.	URL	Uniform Resource Locator which is a set of computer codes used as a reference to data on the Web.
792.	Useable returned questionnaire	A questionnaire which has been completed to an adequate level so that its content may be used as data to assist in answering the research question.

Glossary of Research Concepts and Issues

Valid argument to Vulnerable participants

No.	Term	Definition
793.	Valid argument	An argument which is regarded as having been well presented and well developed and the conclusion of which is accepted as being in some sense correct, at least pro tem.
794.	Validity	The issue as to whether the researcher is actually studying the phenomenon which he or she believes he or she is doing. There are various forms of validity including content validity, ex-ant validity, ex-post validity, face validity, etc.
795.	Value free research	The notion that a researcher can completely disassociate him or herself from their value system. There is no such a thing as "value free research". It is not possible to disconnect a researcher from his or her past, present and future values. However, it is possible to be aware of one's values and take some steps to

No.	Term	Definition
		minimise the impact or influence they have on the research processes and the research findings and recommendations.
796.	Values	Deeply held beliefs often about issues related to right and wrong and how such issues impact on human behaviour. Values are also a reflection on personal ideas about the world and relationships therein which underpin choices and actions. Therefore, whether a researcher is a positivist or an interpretivist may be seen as a reflection of the value which he or she places on the importance of the different approach to knowledge and understanding. All decisions related to a research project including choice of research question/s, choice of research strategy, research design, etc., are directly affected by the researcher's values. In conducting academic research it is important for researchers to be consciously aware of their values. http://bit.ly/1qK2Inp
797.	Variable	An issue or an idea or a concept which attracts the attention of the researcher. Academic research is normally based on attempting to understand variables and

Glossary of Research Concepts and Issues

No.	Term	Definition
		their relationship to one another and the environment in which they exist.
		There may be dependent and independent variables involved in a research question.
		The researcher often wants to understand how a characteristic or a group of characteristics of some system changes as the independent variable changes. The characteristics are regarded and treated as a variable or set of variables.
798.	Verbatim quotations	This involves using the exact words from an authority as a reference. Some short verbatim quotations are acceptable in academic work, but it is possible to have too many. Verbatim quotations should be accompanied by a page number reference.
799.	Verisimilitude	The appearance of being true or real.
800.	Version control	An issue which arises in data management. When data is being entered into a computer it is critical for the researcher to record exactly the point at which any pauses occur so that data will not be unnecessarily re-entered or omitted. Version control is always a challenge and without adequate attention to this level of detail the research may be invalidated.

Glossary of Research Concepts and Issues

No.	Term	Definition
801.	Video blog (Vlog)	Some researchers use the internet to communicate their ideas, but instead of writing a blog they create videos to express their thoughts. This is sometimes referred to as a Vlog.
802.	Video recording	Interviews and focus group discussions are regularly recoded so that the researcher can obtain an accurate transcript. Video recording has begun to replace audio recording. It is important to note that permission should be acquired for such an activity in the letter of consent.
803.	Vignette	A short description or summary of an event or a phenomenon encountered by the research. They may be used to illustrate a concept or to throw light on a situation.
804.	Virtual world	Also known as massive multiplayer online worlds (MMOWs), software products which were developed for entertainment purposes, but which may also be used in research environments.
805.	Viva Voce	Latin term used in the UK for the oral exam which is described as a defence in the USA. The viva is normally used as part of the doctoral examination although it is sometimes also used for masters and bachelor degrees.
806.	VLOG	The shorten form of Video BLOG.

Glossary of Research Concepts and Issues

No.	Term	Definition
		See *Video Blog*
807.	Volunteer sampling	The use of volunteers to collect data. This practice would not be considered sound if the researcher attempts to use statistical methods based on such data for the purposes of inference.
808.	Voyage of discovery	Academic research, especially when it is undertaken for a doctorate, is often described as a voyage of discovery. The main reason for this is that the "ultimate destination" of the research is sometimes not known when the research process is started. Even when the researcher is confident of the so-called "ultimate destination" it often transpires that the research will lead the researcher somewhere else. It is worth keeping in mind Marcel Proust's comment on the voyage of discovery in his work Search of Lost Time: *"The real voyage of discovery consists not in seeking new landscapes, but in having new eyes."*
809.	Vulnerable participants	Individuals who participate as knowledge informants who may be unable to assess whether their participation could be deleterious to their own personal interests. Vulnerable participants include children, the elderly, as well as individuals who are disabled in any way. Some researchers have argued that all employees who provide data or

Glossary of Research Concepts and Issues

No.	Term	Definition
		evidence about the environment in which they work are ultimately vulnerable.

Warranted assertions to Writing style

No.	Term	Definition
810.	Warranted assertions	A term used by pragmatist researchers to describe a research finding in which some credence may be placed.
811.	Webinar	The online equivalent of a seminar.
812.	Weak argument	An argument where the evidence is questionable and the logic used is not well argued.
813.	Weak theory	Weak theory will generally be regarded as not well focused; not important; having little or no discussion of logical arguments in support of the theory; having no grounding; having poorly motivated hypotheses.
814.	Weighting (or weight allocating)	Assigning relative importance to particular issues. Weighting is sometimes used in an attempt to distinguish the relative importance of data obtained from different sources.
815.	What-if analysis	A form of sensitivity analysis which allows researchers to understand the

Glossary of Research Concepts and Issues

No.	Term	Definition
		importance of particular variables in models and paradigms.
		See *Sensitivity analysis*
816.	Wiki	A software product which allows a number of individuals to contribute their understanding of a subject through a shared website.
817.	WhatsApp	A cross-platform messaging and voice over IP service allowing users to inter alia send text and voice messages as well as make calls and share images.
818.	Wikipedia	An online encyclopaedia which academics generally regard as being of limited value. In fact, it is an important source of information for many research projects. It is however important that any information found in Wikipedia be checked for its validity.
819.	Withdrawal from the study	The letter of consent which research participants need to sign is required to point out that the participant may withdraw from the research project at any time and that any data or evidence which he or she has supplied may be removed.
		It is accepted that this is a necessary condition. It is also recognised that such a withdrawal could have a severely negative impact on a research project.

Glossary of Research Concepts and Issues

No.	Term	Definition
820.	Withdrawal of degree	Universities reserve the right to withdraw a degree from a graduate if it is discovered that the basis on which the degree was awarded was falsified by the degree candidate. For example, the discovery that a research dissertation submitted by the degree candidate was written by someone else. http://www.cmu.edu/policies/documents/DegreeWithdraw.html
821.	Word blindness	In proof reading their own work researchers are often incapable of detecting their own errors. This phenomenon is sometimes referred to as word blindness.
822.	Working paper	A paper written to almost formal publication standard that is published in a relatively informal journal. Working papers are often reviewed, but the standards applied are not as strict as for a peer reviewed academic journal.
823.	Working title	It can take a considerable time for the title of a research degree dissertation to be finally settled. However, it is necessary from the outset to have some idea of the research project and this is achieved by having a working title which will probably change.
824.	Writing style	Academic output requires a formal writing style that avoids the use of claims that might to lead to misunderstandings

Glossary of Research Concepts and Issues

No.	Term	Definition
		or exaggerations. Academic writing attempts to be as precise as possible avoiding any degree of ambiguity.

X, Y, Z

X-axis to Z-Score

No.	Term	Definition
825.	X-axis	The horizontal axis on an X-Y graph.

No.	Term	Definition
826.	Y-axis	The vertical axis on an X-Y graph.
827.	Yin and Yang	An ancient Chinese concept to describe the interaction of opposites.
828.	Youtube	A repository of primarily video on an extraordinarily wide range of subjects, a number of which may be useful to academic researchers.

No.	Term	Definition
829.	Zeitgeist	A German expression which is best described as the spirit of the age. The spirit of the age is a term which suggests that it is possible to identify the characteristics of a period of time and distinguish them from how it felt to be in another time period. The spirit of the

	age can have a geographical orientation. Thus the spirit of the age in South Africa under apartheid was to find differences between people and to suggest that harmony between given race groups was only possible by using repressive laws which restricted access between people. The spirit of the post-apartheid age is the opposite.
830. Z-score	A statistical measure of the number of standard deviations a data point is from the average of the sample.

www.ingramcontent.com/pod-product-compliance
Lightning Source LLC
Chambersburg PA
CBHW060501090426
42735CB00011B/2073